For my grandchildren Lilith and Elias

Foreword

On January 03, 2009, the time had come. A new technology saw the light of day: a digital, decentralized monetary system. But what has it meant for society? And why is it so important not to have missed the boat here? These are the questions this book will explore.

However, one thing in advance: this book does not aim to lecture while getting bogged down in technical details. The goal is to help you make up your own mind. Is there any truth to this Bitcoin and blockchain revolution? Or are we, as star investor Warren Buffett once said, just dealing with "rat poison" after all?

On this reading tour, we will together explore whether Bitcoin and blockchain technology have the potential to make entire economic sectors and operations better, faster, more efficient as well as cheaper. We will also take a look at Ethereum - the second largest cryptocurrency after Bitcoin. We will then weigh in on whether it makes sense to enter these areas as an investor. Maybe we'll discover the new Amazon or Google together - in the sense of an investment?

One thing is certain: blockchain technology already enables the global exchange of money, value and contracts. Nothing new, you think? Yes, it is, because with blockchain technology, this exchange works without being dependent on third parties and intermediaries. People can benefit from this on many levels; from private individuals to large companies.

Reason enough to dive into this area in simple and understandable language. Without bells and whistles, but not without loss of information.

Due to its decentralization, it can give people back some of their freedom and self-determination: from corporations, states and banks. An opportunity that should be seized.

This book is intended to help all those who want to use this opportunity as an investment. With practical tips for entering the world of cryptocurrencies and the necessary background knowledge to not be left behind in the next technological revolution.

Especially, because with new and complex technologies, the "Golden Investor Rule" applies more than ever: NEVER invest in businesses of which you do not at least understand the basic concepts. Everybody has to make up his or her own mind about the chances involved before he or she makes an investment!

And by the way: because we are dealing with such a new and ever-changing technology, the electronic version of this book will be updated regularly. Furthermore, since a lot of technical terms, articles and reports are in English, you will find both languages in this book.

But for now, enjoy your reading!

Yours

Maximilian Erlmeier

1. Money Rules the World

Whether you have it or not, you can't get around it: money. It is the glue that holds the world together. However, this cement is neither fair nor particularly reliable. While the rich and powerful divide the fortune and the world-wide wealth among themselves, a majority of the people gets only a very small piece of the cake! The unequal distribution of the world-wide prosperity inevitably leads to poverty and exploitation of many in favor of the luxury and wealth of a few.

The numbers speak for themselves: in a 2017 study, it was found that approximately 1 percent of the world's population owns roughly half of the world's wealth, while the poorer half owns only 1 percent of that wealth. This means that a few people have more money in their hands than they can spend in their entire lives.

In September 2021, for example, Jeff Bezos, founder of Amazon, is considered the richest man in the world with an estimated fortune of $189.2 billion. He employs 18,000 workers in Germany alone. And they earn between 11.30 and 12.70 euros gross per hour as a starting salary. An average worker would therefore have to work 1.7 million years without interruption or sleep to reach the fortune of his or her top boss.

This small glimpse into the pockets of the richest man in the world shows the absurdity of the monetary system well: the money of this world is unfairly distributed.

But this is not only due to the profit maximization of the rich and beautiful. It also has a good deal to do with the fact that very few people still have an overview of how money is created and distributed in the first place, who has power over it and how decisions are made.

This is because the central banks of this world, in cooperation with the states, can print money almost unhindered and thus increase the amount of money in circulation relatively arbitrarily.

The same applies to the banks, which can create money out of thin air by granting loans. This, in turn, results in money losing more and more of its value through inflation. The consequences are well known: prices rise, but wages often do not increase to the same extent.

The fatal consequences of such a monetary policy can be seen in South America's Venezuela. There, the inflation rate in 2020 was 2,355 percent. In August 2021, the country's monetary guardians decided to delete six zeros from all prices, as the many zeros made accounting in that country massively more difficult.

The economic consequences of this high inflation are fatal. As the Venezuelan Bolívar continues to be devalued, people cannot be sure that their money will still be worth at the end of the day what it may have been in the morning.

Inflation is so strong in Venezuela that money loses value so quickly that by the end of the week it may be worth only a fraction of what it was at the beginning of the week.

Saving money has become impossible, and life is getting harder with every new day. Food, gasoline and affordable medicine have become increasingly rare. In their desperation, people are once again resorting to barter, because here they find more security than with the failed state currency. Those who are able to, secure their few possessions or even assets abroad before they are no longer worth anything. Some Venezuelans have already discovered the "digital gold" called Bitcoin for themselves. Although the cryptocurrency itself is not yet stable in value, for many it is more attractive than the Bolívar.

But before we explore why Bitcoin is becoming the increasingly attractive money alternative in Venezuela, we need to ask: How could it have come this far?

Money - The Core Element of a Functioning Society

So let's dive into the history of money to understand what slips through our fingers every day and what we actually use to pay for our sandwiches, coffee and pleasures.

The oldest precursors of money go back to the oldest history of mankind. Our ancestors already used various goods - such as shells, teeth or even cloth - to exchange them for other goods. As early as 20,000 years ago, Western Europeans are said to have paid with small stone axes to buy some meat from other tribes.

Nearly 4,000 years ago, people in Africa began using cowrie snail shells as a medium of exchange. According to tradition, "cowrie money" was used and recognized halfway around the world. As a result, people gave it the most important function of money: it could store value. Because people trusted that for a certain number of the shells they could get a certain amount of a commodity. Thus, cowrie money fulfilled the important monetary function as a "store of value."

In addition, they were forgery-proof - only the shells collected in the Maldives and around the Gulf of Thailand were recognized as cowrie. They were also used as a unit of account; one received a certain amount of goods for a certain amount of shells.

> **Cowrie money is considered one of the first forms of money. The shells of cowries already fulfilled important characteristics: they were used as an account unit, served as a store of value, and were relatively counterfeit-proof.**

Nevertheless, the decorative shells were not a rare commodity, for those who collected them also found them. Thus, cowrie money met the same fate that would befall the Venezuelan Bolívar centuries later.

Over time, people collected so many shells that inflation set in. The cowrie money became more and more worthless, since it was not really scarce anymore, at least, after the transport possibilities had become better and, thus, the small shells could spread all over the world. Eventually, people stopped using the shells as currency in South Asia in the 19th century, and in West Africa at the beginning of the 20th century.

From Shells to Coins - Money is Refined

Coin money had meanwhile become more practical: in the 7th century B.C. in Asia Minor, Ionians and Lydians began to press an alloy of gold and silver in the form of lumps, decorating them with images. The first coins made of pure gold or silver were created in the middle of the 6th century under King Croesus of Lydia. Subsequently, it became all confusing, with all sorts of kings starting to mint their own coins.

The Specter of Inflation

The first paper money finally emerged in tenth-century China. In the Sichuan region, people had previously used coins made of iron. But these were too heavy and too costly to produce; the metal and labor were more expensive than the exchange value. Moreover, in 933, a siege led to a scarcity of coins, so that some merchants decided to issue paper money. Subsequently, the city took over regulating the issuance of paper money until finally, in 1016, the Chinese State took over the issue of banknotes. Thereby, the first nationalization of paper money was accomplished. However, it did not take long for rulers to take advantage of paper money. Various emperors printed money again and again at will, without taking care to maintain its purchasing power. By increasing the money supply in this way, they devalued purchasing power, and massive inflation occurred over and again.

Gold as an Incorruptible Money Anchor

Yet, during the Second World War, a total of 44 nations, including China, Soviet Russia and Great Britain began to work under the auspices of the USA on a system aimed at creating an international monetary order with the U.S. dollar as the reserve currency.

With he so-called Bretton Woods Agreement, the "gold standard" was finally adopted. It was thereby established that each ounce of gold was worth 35 U.S. dollars. This meant that all currencies could take their cue from the U.S. dollar and be confident that something was actually deposited for the paper on which seemingly arbitrary numbers were printed: gold!

This gave an invaluable security: It should no longer be possible to print unlimited money without being oriented to a fixed deposited value, namely that of gold. This is hard to mine, limited, scarce and difficult to manipulate - important characteristics for a monetary anchor!

The Bretton Woods Agreement established gold as a monetary anchor to create a uniform "gold standard."

The Federal Reserve Bank, the central bank of the United States, solemnly promised to buy gold at the specified price in any amount.

In return, the other member states pledged to keep fluctuations in their currencies low.

To oversee the whole thing, the countries set up the International Monetary Fund (IMF), among others. Together with the International Bank for Reconstruction and Development (IBRD), the organizations were to ensure that the agreed rules were adhered to.

At first, the idea seemed ingenious: the precious metal gold became the incorruptible monetary anchor on which the world's most important currencies were based, with the U.S. dollar leading the way as the world's reserve currency. However, the book you are reading right now might never have been necessary, if the idea had lasted. The outcome was forseeable: The Bretton Woods Agreement failed and the gold standard crumbled to dust.

The End of "Gold Money"

By 1969 it became clear that this system was no longer working. At that point, France wanted to exchange its U.S. dollars into gold, but the United States did not have enough gold on hand to keep its promise. So two years later, the United States cancelled its commitment, and the system collapsed. By 1973, Bretton Woods was completely discontinured. Henceforth, there were to be no more fixed exchange rates and so there was no longer a guarantee to be able to exchange one's money at hedged prices.

In the course of these events, gold was to acquire a new function in the global financial market. The precious metal became a new asset class that brought with it important functions. Among other things, it was supposed to protect against inflation and serve to build up wealth. Gold proved to be particularly stable against the U.S. dollar.

While inflation in the USA rose to unimagined heights in the following years, the reserve currency gradually became worthless.

The price of an ounce of gold, on the other hand, rose to over 500 percent of its previous value between the years 1970 and 1979.

After the price of gold was no longer pegged to the U.S. dollar, it became more valuable against the U.S. dollar over time. The precious metal became an asset class in its own right.

For many people, this brought with it the realization that you can solve problems with the money press. The U.S. had tried - uncontrolled printing of new bills was supposed to give the economy a decent boost. But inflation rose and gold, which in contrast cannot be multiplied infinitely, became more and more valuable.

Trust - the Hardest Currency in the World

For those who have read these pages carefully so far, it will have dawned on you: The basis of money is trust. 4,000 years ago, people trusted that they would get a meal for a handful of shells. Later, this promise of being able to exchange money for something was scribbled on paper and weighed in gold with the U.S. dollar.

We trust that the bill or coin we hold in our hand has value in return. If we want to exchange it, we get something in return. We can use it to go to the bakery for a cup of coffee or to a restaurant for a meal. We can buy services or even a car with it.

The problem is that trust in money and the institutions that are responsible for it has been disappointed time and again, and gradually gets squandered.

Let's recall the year 2008. The USA was facing an economic catastrophe. The real estate bubble - triggered by bad loans - burst. This was followed by one bank crash after the next. The money that the banks had lent so generously in the previous period could no longer be repaid. The financial crisis finally culminated in the investment bank Lehman Brothers filing for bankruptcy on September 15, 2008.

People lost their homes and much of their savings, and the crisis spread. Global trade had collapsed, and there was no longer any confidence in the banks. This was followed by the so-called "bank run."

People rushed to the banks to withdraw their savings. But the banks had more and more trouble explaining what they were doing, because some of the money they were supposed to be holding could no longer be paid out. Then the states had to step in. They saved the banks from insolvency, and some were rescued directly with state aid. Many people thought that was unfair. The banks had speculated and society had to foot the bill!

Conclusion: Our monetary and financial system is sick

We remember Jeff Bezos and his associates, the greed of the emperors, inflation, burst loans and speculation by banks. We remember how in Venezuela and many other countries' money is no longer worth anything and now we know why: the international monetary system has broken. The seemingly arbitrary issuance of new money and a lack of an anchor, comparable to gold, clearly shows us that it is difficult to trust in the current monetary systems.

But we are now facing a new upheaval, half a century after the dissolution of the gold standard and the Bretton Woods Agreement. For there has been a digital version of gold since 2009: Bitcoin.

The system behind it cannot be manipulated and is counterfeit-proof as well as protected against inflation. Like gold, it is mined - but in the digital realm. In addition, digital gold has another important property: It is scarce! The maximum amount is limited to 21 million Bitcoin (BTC).

> **Bitcoin (BTC) is counterfeit-proof, cannot be manipulated, is protected against inflation and is scarce. Like gold, it is mined, but the maximum quantity is limited to 21 million units.**

For those who have seen from the above that we need a hedge against inflationary monetary systems, there is no getting around Bitcoin. As the digital successor to gold and the incorruptible money anchor for the various currencies that exist in the world, Bitcoin has the potential to shake up the financial system.

And so we return to Venezuela again: where the state currency has long since lost its trust and its value storage function, people are increasingly trusting that Bitcoin can 'store' value. Better even: as it momentarily looks, the digital currency can even increase value in the long run.

Reason enough to dive into the world of digital gold and take a look at what its ingenious inventor Satoshi Nakamoto has created.

2. Problem and Solution: The Next Big Revolution?

Bitcoin brings with it many features that allow it to cure the ills of our current financial system. There are no central institutions that can distribute the digital currency at will because Bitcoin is backed only by computer code. Moreover, Bitcoin is scarce, the maximum amount is limited, and it brings with it the possibility of not only storing value, but actually increasing it. This monetary system was first published in 2008 by the unknown creator under the pseudonym Satoshi Nakamoto in an anonymous mailing list.

Digital and Decentralized: The Solution!

The big difference that Bitcoin offers to conventional currencies such as the U.S. dollar, the Euro and the like: Bitcoin is decentralized. This means that it does not need a central institution such as a bank to function. Instead, with the Bitcoin network, we are dealing with a distributed system.

We can think of it roughly as a giant spider web that spans the globe. At the nodes (full nodes) of this network are computers that are connected to all the other nodes of the network. There is no center, it is de-centralized. This technology, in which information is provided and stored in a decentralized manner, is called distributed ledger technology. Decentralized systems make it possible to circumvent an important attack surface of centralized systems: The so-called "single point of failure." Because the systems are distributed, there are no individual servers that unwelcome attackers could attack.

Trust in a network?

But how can a network be trusted? It's simple: The full nodes constantly coordinate with each other and follow the set of rules that Satoshi Nakamoto came up with in his white paper.

This creates an agreement - in Bitcoin jargon, this is also referred to as "consensus". Anyone who wants to send Bitcoin (we are talking about "transactions" here) must follow these rules, otherwise the transactions will not be accepted.

> **The Bitcoin network follows set rules: it consists of a decentralized network of computers that ensure that these rules are followed.**

The genius of it all is that all transactions that take place are stored in a chain of data blocks, a blockchain. Each transaction is assigned a complicated mathematical code. Once a block is attached to the blockchain, there is nothing that can be done about it.

Incidentally, anyone in the world can publicly view all transactions that have ever been made on the Bitcoin blockchain. However, one can only see at what time and from which Bitcoin address the data packets were sent. The people behind the transactions remain hidden.

Decentralized and incorruptible? But safe!

> **The Bitcoin network is a blockchain. The various nodes use fixed codes to ensure that every Bitcoin transfer (transaction) follows the same rules. Anyone can check this, making the technology secure and unchangeable or incorruptible.**

Since the Bitcoin network is based on cryptography, it is also referred to as a cryptocurrency. And because the blockchain consists of computers distributed all over the world, we refer to the network as decentralized.

So Bitcoin solves the trust issue in a clever way. Instead of having to trust states and banks, in the Bitcoin network you place your trust in a bombproof technology. But what is this trust worth?

Satoshi Nakamoto and the triumph of Bitcoin

Ever since Bitcoin has been around, the cryptocurrency has been on a breathtaking triumphant march. It has become more and more valuable. In the beginning, however, it was still hard to get anything at all for this digital money.

The "pizza story" shows most impressively how difficult it was and how crazy the Bitcoin story is.

Two Bitcoin Pizzas Worth Billions

The year is 2010, it is May. A certain Laszlo Hanyecz offers 10,000 Bitcoins in an online forum for someone to deliver him two pizzas. His only condition: "Nothing weird with fish or anything!".

It would take a few days before someone took pity on him. But eventually Hanyecz was able to trade in his pizzas and go down in Bitcoin history. Today, among Bitcoiners, May 22 is celebrated as "Pizza Day" - one of the first-ever transactions with the cryptocurrency.

Just eleven years later, those 10,000 Bitcoins would have been worth $570 million. In retrospect, probably the most expensive pizzas in the world. Hanyecz thus did the crypto world a great service. For he was the first to make it possible for Bitcoin to be exchanged for goods. Only through this did an equivalent value enter the Bitcoin circulation. (You can read more about how Bitcoin gets value in the next chapter).

Historical Bitcoin Exchange Rate Development

The price development of the Bitcoin resembles a roller coaster ride. Thus, the cryptocurrency can fluctuate by as much as 90 percent within a year. And that's in both directions. Within less than 10 years, the price of one Bitcoin climbed from under one cent to just under $20,000 (at the end of 2017), only to plummet back to $3,000 a short time later in 2018. But even from there, it went steeply uphill: as early as April 2021, the Bitcoin price reached its peak of 60,000 US dollars.

What is stable about it, however, is that it has been constantly going up for years. A look at the past shows that every person who invested in Bitcoin and waited four years is in the black. And anyone who waited eight years is rich today!

The Value of the Bitcoin

The Bitcoin price is calculated according to the principle of supply and demand. This means that if I want to sell a Bitcoin, it is worth as much as someone else is willing to pay for it. "So far so good," you may think, "that's the way it is with all commodities." But Bitcoin is a bit different.

That's because the beauty of Bitcoin is that the supply is limited. For there is only a certain amount of Bitcoins. There will be a maximum of 21 million in total. (This has to do with a process called "mining". But we will get to that later).

So the cryptocurrency "Bitcoin" becomes more valuable with each new "Bitcoiner" (i.e. people who own BTC). To illustrate this, let's imagine a delicious cake - the big Bitcoin cake. Now this cake is so delicious that a great many people in the world want to try it. However, there are not so many pieces of cake in total! That's why the individual pieces become more and more valuable and are divided into smaller and smaller pieces.

> **The Bitcoin number is limited. There will be a maximum of 21 million Bitcoin. If demand continues to develop as it has in recent years, it will become more and more valuable.**

By the way, you don't have to buy a whole Bitcoin to get a piece of the pie. You can also buy fractions, such as 0.0001 BTC. The decimal places are called Satoshi as is the inventor of the cryptocurrency.

The digital gold

Now we know that there is only a certain number of Bitcoin and that the individual Bitcoins are becoming more and more valuable. This is because more and more people trust that this is a precious commodity. That's why it's increasingly being referred to as "digital gold." And that has to do with its origins, among other things.

Bitcoins are mined in a similar way to gold. However, not in real mines, but in the digital realm. In English, this is referred to as "mining". The people (or rather computers) who mine the Bitcoins are called miners.

> **The process of creating Bitcoin is called mining. Those who "mine" Bitcoin are rewarded with Bitcoin.**

In the process, they compete and have to solve complicated arithmetic problems. After all, they have to abide by the rules so that the blockchain can remain secure. If they solve the tasks successfully, they are allowed to add another block to the blockchain. They are ultimately rewarded for their efforts. For each successfully mined block in the blockchain, they get a certain amount of Bitcoin (currently 6.25 BTC).

Bitcoin versus Gold

The similarities between Bitcoin and gold are obvious. Both are mined, one digitally, the other analog. In addition, both serve as a store of value and therefore are a hedge of wealth. More and more people are turning to Bitcoin to protect their wealth against inflation and loss of value, just as people do with gold.

In the meantime, however, there are initial indications that Bitcoin could even be the better gold. The main reason for this is scarcity. This is because the maximum Bitcoin quantity is, we remember, set at 21 million units. The distribution of new Bitcoins is fixed in the blockchain and can thus be calculated precisely. New Bitcoins are mined at regular intervals, currently 6.25 BTC per block. The amount of new Bitcoins is also regularly halved.

During the so-called "halving", which takes place every four years, the supply of new Bitcoins is artificially halved. This artificial supply shortage ultimately has an impact on the value placed on Bitcoin: A rare commodity that is becoming increasingly valuable.

With gold, on the other hand, the matter is not so clear-cut. Because, in fact, nothing is known exactly about the gold reserves that still lie dormant under the earth. If, for example, someone were to stumble upon a new gold vein completely unexpectedly, this could have a significant impact on the price of gold. Gold could thus meet the fate that we have seen time and again in the history of money. A sharp increase in the total amount could cause the precious metal to unexpectedly lose value. 1:0 for Bitcoin.

Bitcoin - the Perfect Store of Value

But let's look at Bitcoin's properties as a store of value again. Generally accepted properties of a store of value, apart from scarcity, are transferability, divisibility and durability.

Those who have been paying close attention up to this point will have guessed: The match will be decided in favor of Bitcoin. Because Bitcoin is also streets ahead of its analog predecessor in terms of transferability.

For example, digital coins can be sent around the globe in seconds, whereas we would encounter massive problems with gold bars in such an endeavor. Imagine trying to send a gold bar to acquaintances in another country! Who knows if such a gold shipment would ever arrive? But even if it did: It would then take some time for the glittering metal to reach its destination. With Bitcoin, that happens within seconds.

The cryptocurrency is also more divisible than gold. Or let's say: With less effort. Because when buying Bitcoin, it makes no difference in this context whether we buy 0.000001337 BTC or an entire BTC. With gold it is more difficult - if you want 1.256436 grams of gold, you need a very precise scale.

> **Bitcoin is more divisible and more easily transferable than gold. It is also scarcer.**

Gold also has to admit defeat in terms of durability. Gold jewelry wears out over time, loses its luster, or even its weight. Bitcoin, on the other hand, is made for eternity: chiseled into the blockchain forever.

In one respect, it must be fairly admitted, analog gold is still ahead of Bitcoin. Its millennia of use and recognition have already established it in people's minds. Bitcoin, on the other hand, still has a long way to go. But should more and more people recognize the advantages of digital gold for themselves, this is just another point in favor of putting Bitcoin in one's digital pocket. Because Bitcoin has already had a unique career within 12 years.

"Bitcoin handles it!" - What makes the cryptocurrency unique

Bitcoin is, as we already know, decentralized, digital and tamper-proof. Plus, we can confidently call it the "digital gold." But the cryptocurrency offers even more advantages.

Financial Self-Determination - Be your own bank.

Among Bitcoin enthusiasts, the bon-mot "Be your own bank" is circulating. This slogan is representative of the cryptocurrency, because it theoretically offers anyone with access to the Internet the opportunity to participate in the network.

And this is in complete contrast to the international banking system, in which you hardly have a chance to enter the financial system without a fixed residence and often also without a regular income.

Yet, there is more than enough demand here. According to data from the World Bank, around 1.7 billion people worldwide have no access to the financial sector. This means that almost a quarter of the world's population do not have a bank account and are thus excluded from global trade.

In parts of the African continent in particular, the lack of a freely accessible financial infrastructure presents people with massive problems. Even those who are lucky enough to be supported by relatives from abroad have to give up a large proportion of their money. This is because those who don't have an account, have to resort to large service providers. And the latter often charge high fees.

Bitcoin knows no borders. Anyone with Internet access can send Bitcoin around the world!

But Bitcoin takes care of that. It is already enough to have a digital wallet to send Bitcoin on its journey within a short time. It doesn't matter where the money is going.

This is because the blockchain can be accessed at any time from anywhere in the world - without any branches or financial service providers. Given the sheer number of people without bank accounts, the potential is huge.

Of course, this is not limited to the African continent. With the ability to send censorship- resistant Bitcoins, anyone - including you - can send the digital coins around the world at any time!

Digital Scarcity

The Internet and also our society are known for producing everything in abundance. Be it consumer goods, food or even data on the Internet; there is so much of most things in the Western countries that one can hardly imagine the numbers.

It is no different with money. Central banks can print new money almost at will; the amount of money in circulation can be increased at the push of a button. This is at the expense of society. Because when more money is printed, in most cases it leads to inflation. This, in turn, means that people get less for their money and their purchasing power falls. And society has hardly any influence on or overview of how much money the central banks print.

Not so with Bitcoin. Because in this monetary system there will ever be a maximum of 21 million Bitcoins, after that it's over. Currently (as of October 2021), there are 18.84 million Bitcoins in circulation. Experts even speak here of the scarcest commodity of mankind! The cryptocurrency thus offers a counter-design to ordinary money. In contrast to the Euro, US dollar and Co., the distribution is deflationary.

This also means that - assuming demand remains constant - Bitcoin will become more and more valuable.

> **Bitcoin is digital, decentralized, censorship resistant and deflationary.**

Bitcoin is also independent. No ban by states or regulators has the power to shut down the blockchain. It is a clockwork that keeps turning. This also makes the cryptocurrency safe from manipulation. The only law Bitcoin is subject to is computer code. Among Bitcoiners, the motto "Code is law" therefore applies.

Big Ideas - Powerful Enemies

"First they ignore you, then they laugh at you, then they fight you, and then you win."

This quote by Mahatma Gandhi in the context of the peaceful revolution in India translates well to Bitcoin. Because at first the cryptocurrency was not noticed at all, then later it was ridiculed. At some point, states tried to ban it, but failed. And today? It's quite possible that the peaceful Bitcoin revolution will win in the end. We will see. Personally, however, I am hopeful and, like many other Bitcoiners, will work hard to make it happen.

This is due because Satoshi Nakamoto's Bitcoin project has big ambitions. With a decentralized, digital money system, it offers an alternative to the current financial system. This system is losing more and more trust among people, but still has the big players on its side. be it central banks or major banks, corporations, digital monopolists or states like the USA. Yet, Bitcoin has the potential to take on the established financial system.

It offers an alternative for all those who fall out of the current monetary system. To participate in the Bitcoin network, you don't need much except access to the Internet. At the same time, it creates the possibility of sending money around the world in seconds. And it does so with far lower fees than Western Union and the like.

Moreover, with each passing day, it is establishing itself more and more as a store of value that can protect people from losing the purchasing power of their own assets. If you store your money in Bitcoin, there is a good chance that after a few years (or even in just a few months) it will be significantly more valuable than in your bank account. Just think of the bad habit of banks to introduce penalty interest rates! Whereas in the past you were rewarded with interest if you deposited your money in a bank, now you have to pay for it. Not so with Bitcoin.

The Crucial Questions

Public perception of Bitcoin and blockchain technology fluctuates. Some call it the greatest opportunity of the century, others a pyramid scheme and huge scam.

But it is best to judge for yourself. And, to judge for yourself, the most important foundation is to be well informed. For the following chapters, I suggest three guiding questions for you to keep in mind.

1. Is blockchain a "disruptive technology" that offers a superior model to current methods? (We're talking primarily about the application areas of money transfer, business processing, anti-counterfeiting, and secure contracts.)

2. Will Bitcoin with its scarcity, similar to gold, become an important store of value and a new asset class, so that it can be considered a safe haven in times of crisis?

3. Does cryptocurrency have the potential to give people back some independence and freedom from banks and states? Does Bitcoin offer an alternative for people without own banking access?

If you answer "yes" to these questions after reading this book, then it might be a good idea to get into it. And not just mentally, but perhaps with manageable investments.

3. Knowledge, Facts & Figures

If you want to answer all these questions for yourself, you must of course know what is being talked about. Coin, bitcoin network, blockchain, nodes, cryptography and so on are still foreign words for you? No problem.

On the following pages we will clarify together the most important terms around Bitcoin. As simple as possible and only as complicated as necessary! Because only if the basic terms are clear and the connections are understood, you can understand and appreciate the genius and groundbreaking of Satoshi Nakamoto's idea. With a new technology, it's like with a foreign language: without learning a little vocabulary, nothing works.

However, it will be well worth it. The better you understand the key terms, the more informed you can be in assessing the opportunities and risks of Bitcoin and this new technology called blockchain.

The Triumph of Distributed Ledger Technologies

"Distributed Ledger" can initially be translated as a distributed ledger of accounts. Distributed ledger technology is therefore a decentralized database. This means that it allows network participants to access the database collectively. Sound familiar already? Very well. Because the Bitcoin network, as a blockchain, is a particular form of distributed ledger technology.

One of the things that makes such distributed accounts special is that it doesn't require a central authority to grant access. Rather, individual participants can add records without the need for an institution such as a bank to allow it. The network always updates itself, so all participants always have the most current version of the database. The rules are set in the network, which itself ensures that they are adhered to. Certain consensus mechanisms such as "proof of work" or "proof of stake" are used for this purpose.

The Bitcoin blockchain is a specific type of distributed ledger technology.

Depending on the area of application, such distributed ledgers can be designed differently. If, as with the Bitcoin blockchain, one is dealing with open access for everyone, one speaks of an "unpermissioned" ledger. If, however, you want to restrict access to a specific group of people, we speak of "permissioned" ledgers.

This makes sense, for example, if a company only wants to share certain sensitive information with a selected group of people, such as its own employees.

By eliminating the need to go through intermediaries and central institutions, distributed ledger technologies can save a lot of time and money, especially in industry. Popular areas of application for the technology include logistics, the automotive industry and the energy sector.

Basic Terms - in a Nutshell

Address: the Bitcoin address is similar to the account number at banks. It can be used to send and receive BTC.

All-time high: refers to the highest price ever paid for an asset. Bitcoin's all-time high is $64,805.00 and was recorded on 04/14/2021.

Altcoin: is a portmanteau of "alternative" and "coin" and refers to all other cryptocurrencies except Bitcoin.

Asset(s): are usually stocks, foreign exchange and real estate. However, cryptocurrencies such as Bitcoin are also referred to as assets.

Bear market refers to a market phase in which prices tend to fall. The sentiment among investors is "bearish."

Bitcoin (BTC): is the best known and oldest cryptocurrency. It was developed by Satoshi Nakamoto.

Bitcoin ATM: A Bitcoin ATM is a machine where you can exchange BTC for fiat money.

Block: A block is a part of a blockchain. Each block contains important information about transactions on the network.

Blockchain: the blockchain is the technological foundation of Bitcoin. To be precise, Bitcoin is a blockchain. The blockchain is a kind of digital book that contains information about transactions.

Block reward: is the reward that miners get for keeping the Bitcoin network running. It currently consists of 6.25 BTC and transaction fees.

Borrowing: the lending of cryptocurrencies, for which you get money. (See also "Lending").

Bull Market: is the counterpart of the bear market. Prices are rising and sentiment is "bullish".

Centralization: centralized systems have a fixed center. Especially in computer networks, this creates vulnerabilities that attackers can exploit.

Collateral: amount in a specific cryptocurrency that one deposits as collateral when borrowing money in the decentralized finance (DeFi) space.

Cold Wallet: is considered a safe way to store one's Bitcoins. In this case, the necessary information is stored offline.

DApp: is analogous to an app on smartphones - is a program that runs on decentralized networks.

Decentralization: describes the basic principle behind Bitcoin. Instead of a central hub such as a bank, Bitcoin consists of a network of computers distributed around the world. The system is decentralized.

Decentralized Finance (DeFi): describes all decentralized applications that have formed around Bitcoin & Co. in the field of finance.

Distributed Ledger Technology (DLT): are decentralized systems, which include the Bitcoin blockchain.

Double Spending: describes the possibility of spending digital money twice. This problem is solved in Bitcoin by the proof-of-work consensus mechanism.

Ethereum: is the second largest blockchain project in the crypto space. It focuses on "smart contracts," or programmable contracts. The associated cryptocurrency is called Ether (ETH).

ERC-20 token: is the token standard on the Ethereum blockchain.

Fear of Missing Out (FOMO): describes the fear of missing out. Investor sentiment that leads to rash actions.

Fear, Uncertainty and Doubt (FUD): refers to a combination of fear, uncertainty and doubt. Basic attitudes that tempt investors to sell their assets in a hurry in an unsettled market situation.

Fiat(money): From lat: fiat = "let there be". Term for traditional currency such as the U.S. dollar, Euro or Chinese Yuan.

Fungibility: describes the property of monetary units to be interchangeable.

Futures: ability to make bets for future price events.

Genesis block: the first block in the blockchain.

Halving: the "bitcoin halving" occurs approximately every four years. During this process, the supply of new BTC is cut in half.

Trading volume: the amount of goods traded in a given period of time. Gives an indication of how widespread a particular (crypto) currency or asset is.

Hash: digital fingerprint responsible for security in the Bitcoin network, among other things.

Hash Rate: the hash rate measures the computing power in networks such as Bitcoin.

Hodl: is a trendy word in crypto slang. "Hodlers" hold Bitcoin for an indefinite period of time without selling them. They "hodl."

Hot wallet: way to store cryptocurrencies online.

Initial Coin Offering (ICO): describes an event where a new cryptocurrency or token is issued. (In reference to the initial public offering (IPO) on the traditional stock exchange).

Initial Public Offering (IPO): event in which a company goes public, issuing shares.

Know Your Customer (KYC): requirement for crypto exchanges to verify the identity of their customers.

Consensus Mechanism: is the means by which participants in a network come to agreement ("consensus").

Crypto Lending Ability: to lend one's crypto assets to generate further income.

Cryptography Encryption technique: allows information to be transmitted in secret.

Cryptocurrency: digital currency that has cryptography as its basis.

Lending: is the lending of cryptocurrencies in exchange for depositing collateral.

Lightning Network: a network designed to make payments with bitcoin faster.

Liquidity: having sufficient liquidity means having enough "liquid" money to meet payment obligations.

Market capitalization describes the amount of money a cryptocurrency has in total circulation. It is calculated from the token quantity and the current price.

Masternodes: ensure that the Bitcoin network continues to run. They store the entire history of the blockchain.

Mining: is the process by which new Bitcoins "come into the world". In the process, miners ("prospectors") calculate new blocks that are stapled to the blockchain. They receive BTC as a reward for their work.

Mining Difficulty: describes how complicated it is to "mine" new Bitcoins.

Miner: the miners are a network of computers. They solve computational tasks to attach new blocks to the blockchain. In return, they receive the "Block Reward" as a reward.

Mining: the activity of miners (see above).

Mining Farm: is a collection of devices that mine Bitcoin. Usually they are located in halls.

Mining Pool: an association of different devices to mine Bitcoin together.

Mining Reward: the reward for miners. If they find a correct block, they get bitcoins and transaction fees for it.

Intermediary: intermediary between two parties. In finance, for example, banks are the middlemen.

Non Fungible Token (NFT): digital collectibles in token form. They represent shares in famous works of art, for example.

Off chain: a transaction is "off chain" if it is processed outside the blockchain.

Open source: in the case of software, open source means that everyone has access to it.

Paper wallet: a way to keep the digital keys to one's Bitcoins safe.

Peer to Peer: In peer-to-peer networks, participants contact each other directly. They do not need any intermediaries.

Private Key: is a kind of password with which you always have access to your Bitcoins - no matter from where.

Proof of Work: consensus mechanism in the Bitcoin network. Ensures unanimity by proving ("proof") that each party has done work ("work").

Protocol: the network protocol contains the rules by which the network operates.

Pyramid scheme or "Ponzi scheme": is a business model that requires an ever-increasing number of participants to function.

Satoshi: describes the smallest unit in the Bitcoin system. 1 Bitcoin has 100 million satoshis. Satoshis are therefore similar to cents in the Euro, except that there are much larger decimal places.

Satoshi Nakamoto: is the unknown inventor of Bitcoin. Until today nobody knows who Satoshi really is.

Security Token: a digital security.

Security Token Offering (STO): event in which Security Tokens (see above) are issued.

Single Point of failure: refers to a central point of attack; in the case of computer systems, this is often individual servers.

Smart Contract: "Intelligent contract" that is executed automatically as soon as certain events occur.

Stablecoins: are digital coins that represent a fixed, constant value. For example, there are stablecoins that are pegged to the U.S. dollar and accordingly promise value stability to the U.S. currency.

Stock-to-flow ratio: describes the rarity of a good.

Store of Value: is the value promise or the value storage property of a good.

Supply Chain: is a network in which companies are involved in the various processes.

Tether is the best known stablecoin (see above). A Tether (USDT) promises to always be worth one US dollar.

Token is a unit. Owners of a token get certain rights by owning it. This right is classically a payment.

Token Sale: refers to the issuance of new tokens.

Transaction: is similar to a wire transfer and refers to the sending of Bitcoins or other cryptocurrencies.

Transaction Fee: the money you have to pay to make a transaction (see above).

Volatility: describes the price fluctuations of a certain asset, for example Bitcoin. A high volatility means that the price fluctuates a lot.

Whale: a "Bitcoin whale" is a term used to describe people or addresses that own a large amount of BTC.

Wallet: is the digital wallet where you can store cryptocurrencies like Bitcoin.

White Paper: Bitcoin's White Paper contains the technical basics and the basic idea for Bitcoin.

Blockchain yay, Bitcoin nay?

The triumph of blockchain technology sometimes seems almost unstoppable. A growing number of well-known corporations are discovering the advantages of the decentralized technology. Complete work areas, for example in the area of supply chains or even the energy industry, are already being outsourced to blockchain technology. But time and again, especially in Germany, one encounters resistance when it comes to Bitcoin. People are quick to say that the price fluctuations are high, that the technology is not secure, or that it is even used by criminals.

However, what is unfortunately all too often overlooked is the fact that without Bitcoin, blockchain technology would probably not exist in its current form. This is because Bitcoin is the very first and arguably the most famous, and perhaps the most ingenious, use case for blockchain technology.

Therefore, Satoshi Nakamoto's cryptocurrency also takes an important pioneering role, which should not be forgotten in such discussions. And also in terms of price fluctuations, it has to be said so far: in the long run, everyone, who has not sold too early, has still been able to make a profit.

But, it is not just about that. Rather, Bitcoin is also about the possibility of gradually taking some of the power away from the centralized monopolists. And this power should go back to the individual people, those who live and suffer under the centralization and monopolies of this world.

Bitcoin is not an anonymous digital currency

Particularly in media reports, Bitcoin is repeatedly referred to as being anonymous. This, according to the frequent reproachful tone, makes the cryptocurrency particularly suitable for illegal activities.

Money laundering and terror financing - so the ever-repeated accusation - is possible through Bitcoin.

However, these claims are based on a misunderstanding. For Bitcoin, contrary to all claims, is not anonymous. Moreover, Bitcoin is referred to as pseudo-anonymous.

Bitcoin addresses initially consist of a string of letters and numbers, which is why the addresses are also called "alphanumeric". Anyone who looks at Bitcoin transactions on the blockchain therefore only receives information about the time and the amount of the respective transactions.

However, this does not yet allow any conclusion as to who is actually behind the respective transfers. The Bitcoin address can therefore be compared to an IBAN for bank accounts. At first glance, you don't know who is behind it. But with a little effort, authorities can often find out who is behind the addresses.

Bitcoin is not anonymous. Bitcoin is pseudo-anonymous.

Bitcoin exchanges and other trading sites where you can buy Bitcoin in particular are required to follow know-your-customer (KYC) policies. This means that anyone registering on such a platform must register with their full name and address. And this is where the "missing link" between the seemingly anonymous Bitcoin address and the people behind it can be found.

In the past, this has repeatedly led to spectacular search successes by the authorities. Time and again, criminals have fallen under the fallacy that Bitcoin is anonymous. But thanks to the transparency of the blockchain, the authorities were ultimately able to track them down.

Is Bitcoin, proof of work and energy consumption, an insoluble problem?

Anyone who deals with Bitcoin in depth will sooner or later come across the problem of high energy consumption. Calculations by the University of Cambridge, for example, assume that Bitcoin (as of 2021) consumes 88.82 terawatt hours of electricity - roughly 1.5 times that of the entire country of Switzerland. Comparisons such as these settle in the collective memory; they are striking and memorable. One inevitably asks oneself: Is a currency or an asset or an investment allowed to consume so much energy?

> **Bitcoin requires a lot of energy for its consensus mechanism. This ensures security in the network.**

First, we have to look at the reason for Bitcoin's high power consumption. This is fed by the high computing effort that the network operates in order to remain secure. In the so-called proof-of-work consensus mechanism, computers have to solve complicated computational tasks to ensure that only verified transactions are chiseled into the blocks of the blockchain. (For all you pros, this process is highly simplified. Correctly put, the various nodes compete to find a valid block of the block header that is smaller than the Difficulty Target.) This makes it tamper-proof and impossible to manipulate! A feature Bitcoin enthusiasts cite to justify energy consumption. But is that enough?

Critics are quick to object that Bitcoin has hardly been able to establish itself as a means of payment so far, and its mere use to store value hardly justifies such a large energy consumption.

Fundamental questions arise here: where does one get the claim to consume energy? What about credit card companies, gold and silver mining, the arms industry, or air travel by politicians? Doesn't creating a tamper-proof and decentralized cryptocurrency that has the potential to redistribute wealth also have a claim to consume energy? With questions like these, it is already becoming apparent that the energy debate surrounding Bitcoin is a question that everyone must answer for themselves.

An important question, which also often remains untouched, is the question of the origin of the electricity needed for mining. After all, figures on electricity consumption say little about CO2 emissions - and that is what ultimately matters.

Since the field of mining is so confusing and decentralized, only estimates can be given here. CoinShares estimates that about 74 percent of mining electricity comes from renewable energy. Cambridge University, on the other hand, arrives at only 39 percent in a study from 2020.

Renewables or not, the problem is there and everyone needs to face the debate. But the question ultimately boils down to one point: It depends on the added value that one sees in cryptocurrencies and, above all, Bitcoin - or not. For those who see absolutely no point in Bitcoin and have no need to change anything about the current monetary system, Bitcoin's energy consumption will undoubtedly be too high.

However, for those who believe that the financial system in its current form will not last, leads to injustice and that we need an alternative store of value, the energy consumption may be justified. The current monetary system also swallows a lot of energy. The maintenance of the worldwide banks and stock exchanges alone, with countless buildings and millions of employees, eats up massive amounts of energy. If we were to save some of these banks and instead rely on decentralized systems, we could even save energy.

Yet, even for people who are struggling with their own carbon footprint on the one hand, but also want to be part of the Bitcoin network on the other, there are ways to balance things out. The first thing that comes to mind is are projects like www.atmosfair.de. Here, anyone can make a donation to offset CO2 and support projects that save carbon dioxide around the world.

This does not cancel out the CO2 that has already been emitted. Nevertheless, it ensures that the future becomes a little greener. In this way, shares of profits generated by cryptocurrencies can be invested wisely. On top of that, you can reduce your tax burden - because such contributions to CO2 offsetting are treated like conventional donations by the tax office.

You can also take a critical look at your own lifestyle - perhaps you can save a plane trip or a car journey at one point? Are there perhaps unnecessary energy guzzlers that can be saved? If you put the money into an alternative monetary system instead and donate a part of the profits, you have already gained a lot. Not only for yourself, but also for your environment.

Conclusion

Before we go any further, let's pause for a moment. After learning about the history of money and the pitfalls of inflation in the first chapter, we were able to understand in the second chapter that a revolution in the monetary system is about to take place with Bitcoin.

This new digital currency has the ability to store value and that, it appears, even better than gold. In the third chapter, we were able to learn quite a bit about the fundamental technology behind Bitcoin - distributed ledger technology. As such, the Bitcoin blockchain is stepping up to provide a new answer to the question of trust in the monetary system. In the following chapter, things get a bit technical - together we look at Satoshi Nakamoto's legendary "white paper: The Blueprint for Digital Gold", the paper that started the ball rolling.

4. Satoshi Nakamoto's White Paper - The Solution to the Core Issues of a Sound Financial Economy

In his white paper, Satoshi Nakamoto explains the basic features of a monetary system that has it all. Titled "Bitcoin: A Peer-to-Peer Electronic Cash System," he presents the blueprint for a digital currency unlike anything the world had ever known. It is one of the best, clearest, and most basic guides on how people can work against the aberrations in the financial economy. It is definitely worth reading!

And believe it or not, it is only 9 pages long! The problem is that it is a lot to read, and you have to be an expert to get through it. That's why we'll pick out the most important aspects below and try to make them understandable even for non-specialists. Here we go:

Bitcoin: A Peer-to-Peer Electronic Cash System

Even the headline is a bit of a mouthful. A "bit" does not stand for a well-known (German Bitburger) beer brand. Rather, it is a unit of measurement in the field of electronics, the centimeter of computers if you will. "Coin" is the coin. And there we have it: Bitcoin, the electronic coin.

A Bitcoin is an electronic coin.

A "peer-to-peer" network is a network in that the individual participants contact each other directly. They don't need anyone to mediate between them - that's why we call it de-centralized.

That leaves one more thing. The "Electronic Cash System" can be translated as "electronic money system". Money, in other words, that works electronically, unlike our paper money. Putting these three building blocks together, we have also captured the essence of Bitcoin:

> **Bitcoin is an electronic money system built on a peer-to-peer network.**

And further in the text.

> **"Overview. A pure peer-to-peer version of an electronic payment system would allow online payments to be sent from one party directly to another without going through a financial institution."**

Alert readers already know: bitcoin comes without intermediaries. This means that digital money does not require a bank to come between people. Any person in the world ("party") can send money to another person anywhere in the world at any time.

> **"Digital signatures form part of the solution, but the main benefits are lost if a trusted third party is still needed to prevent double spending (multiple spending). We propose a solution to the double-spending problem by using a peer-to-peer network."**

The problem that arises when electronic payments are made without a middleman is called the "double-spending problem." That's because no one can control that individual participants don't spend their money twice. Until now. But Bitcoin regulates that - within the network.

> **"The network timestamps transactions by hashing them into a continuous chain of hash-based proofs of work, creating a record that cannot be changed without recreating the proof of work."**

Nobody can blame you, at this point at the latest, you say, "Huh?". But we can crack this nut as well. Let's take a quick step back and summarize. We have an electronic network of digital coins called

Bitcoins. This network wants to manage without a bank. But now it faces a problem: Who is now checking that people are not simply spending their money twice and three times?

The answer is: the network itself. More specifically, the technology. Even more specifically, blockchain technology. And it works like this:

To make sure everything is correct, the network staples the current time ("timestamp") to each transfer ("transaction") and strings them together, just like a string of pearls. To do this, however, it must provide proof - the so-called "proof of work." Now, when enough transfers are collected, they are packed into a block and hung on the chain. And once a block is on the chain, it can no longer be detached.

The ingenious thing about this is that the longer the chain, the more secure it becomes. That's because each new block contains information about the entire history of all transactions.

"The longest chain serves not only as proof of the sequence of witnessed events, but also as proof that it comes from the largest pool of CPU power."

So with the Bitcoin blockchain, there is only ever one valid version. That's the one with the longest length. This also protects the technology from attackers. Malicious attackers would have to claim over 50 percent of the computing power of the entire network to be able to "crack the chain."

"As long as most of the CPU power is controlled by nodes that don't cooperate to attack the network, they will generate the longest chain and be faster than the attackers. The network itself requires only minimal structure. Messages are transmitted on a best-effort basis, and nodes can leave and re-

enter the network at will, accepting the longest proof-of-work chain as evidence of what happened while they were away."

So now we come to the nodes, in German they can also be referred to as "network nodes." They ensure that the network remains stable and secure. Another ingenious thing about the blockchain: the nodes are not fixed, every person who can muster the necessary energy by means of a computer can also act as a node.

In this sense, you can think of the blockchain as a railroad line with a large number of stations - anyone can get on and ride along for a while. When one gets off again is up to one's own decision.

This is because the blockchain offers any number of connection points to which nodes can dock. Then they just have to work enough and become part of the network. But to do this, they also have to prove that they are working. This proof is called "proof of work."

In doing so, they solve computational problems so complicated that the Bitcoin system is bombproof.

"What's needed is an electronic payment system based on cryptographic proof rather than trust, which allows two willing parties to work directly with each other without the need for a trusted third party."

Only then will it be possible for a monetary system to exist that is completely without a bank or a government. The only thing people need to trust is the technology.

5. Blockchain Technology: The "New Internet"

It's becoming clear by now: bitcoin is solving the trust issue in a new, unprecedented way. As digital gold, the cryptocurrency crosses borders while being open to anyone who wants to become part of the network. And the people who are convinced of the Bitcoin network are becoming more by the day.

Many of these Bitcoin and Blockchain enthusiasts are convinced that the new decentralized technologies will change our society. For example, there are always people who compare the current development of blockchain technology with the Internet of the 1990s.

Back then, people hardly understood how profoundly the Internet would change our society. There were a few visionaries who understood that companies like Amazon, Google, Ebay and Co. would shape the future.

But there were also many who ridiculed or even scoffed at the new technology. Will we feel the same way about blockchain technology? Let's take a closer look at the possibilities offered by the technology.

Blockchain Technology: a Game Changer

To avoid misunderstandings: This chapter will look at blockchain technology per se - this is less about Bitcoin. After all, Bitcoin, in terms of a financial technology, is just one of many use cases for the blockchain.

Nevertheless, it is worth reminding ourselves of some of the advantages that blockchain technology offers in the Bitcoin use case. It is decentralized, cannot be manipulated, is transparent, and does not require intermediaries. It is this latter characteristic that provides it with numerous use cases in industry and society. Below, we take a look at some exemplary ones.

Logistics: Saving Resources and Detours

Logistics is considered a prime example when it comes to applications for blockchain technology. By using decentralized technology, it is possible to increase not only speed but also security when exchanging information. This allows businesses, consumers and suppliers to communicate more efficiently - and they don't need a third party to get in the way!

All parties involved have access to the same information. In addition, the network updates itself as soon as individual participants enter new data. Manipulation or incorrect information is thus a thing of the past.

In addition, logistics companies can rely on "smart contracts" when using blockchain. These are programmable contracts. These are executed as soon as certain events occur.

Healthcare

Blockchain technology can also be used in healthcare. Here, one can most likely rely on "private blockchains." These are set up so that only people who have authorization to do so can access them, for example doctors. The blockchain itself can then be used to store patient data, which doctors can only access if the patient allows them to. The big advantage is that this gives patients themselves more control over what happens to their data.

Whether it's logistics, healthcare, insurance, real estate or the energy sector, blockchain technology can make business processes more efficient and save a lot of time and work.

Insurance

Another potential use case for blockchain technology is insurance. By using the technology, claims can be settled in an automated way. The technology itself can take care of managing the various insurance claims - a way to save billions of money.

Real Estate

Sales of real estate can also be handled using blockchain technology. So-called security tokens can be used to flawlessly acquire ownership of real estate or parts of real estate. By storing them on the blockchain, fraud becomes virtually impossible. Because once recorded on the blockchain, the data can no longer be manipulated.

Energy Sector

The energy market is complicated and confusing. Blockchain technology can provide a remedy here. For example, it can be used to better account for private solar installations. Where the electricity goes and how it is billed can be easily tracked using blockchain.

This was just a small glimpse into the potential uses of blockchain. But it becomes clear - the technology has it all. It can make complete business processes more efficient. Simply by making intermediaries superfluous, it can save unimagined amounts of time and work.

But we are still at the beginning of a major development. This becomes clear when you take a closer look at the typical evolution of technologies.

The Gartner Hype Cycle

The theory of the Gartner hype cycle goes back to analyst Jackie Fenn. Since she published her text "The Microsoft Software Hype Cycle Strikes Again" in 1995, it has been applied to new technologies time and again. It is supposed to help assess the development status of new technologies. It can also be applied to Bitcoin and blockchain technology to get an idea of the current stage of development.

As you can already see from the diagram, the cycle ranks new technologies both from the aspect of (public) attention (Y-axis) and from the aspect of elapsed time (X-axis).

At the beginning of a development there is always the technological trigger - in our case the "birth" of Bitcoin with the Genesis block on January 03, 2009.

This is followed, according to the Gartner hype cycle, by the "peak of inflated expectations." Here we are in a hype phase around the new technology and its offshoots. At the time when the Internet started its revolution, new start-ups were springing up everywhere. As we know today, very few of them had any substance. However, the technology survived.

It was a similar story with Bitcoin and the crypto market in 2017. Suddenly, there were new, seemingly promising projects everywhere, so-called "Initial Coin Offerings." Each of these new projects promised to be the great new technological revolution. People invested blindly until the crypto market formed a huge bubble towards the end of the year, which finally burst. The Bitcoin price fell from its then all-time high of just under $20,000 to a fraction of its level, dragging all the altcoins down with it. We had arrived at phase 3: The Valley of Disappointment.

> **At the end of 2017, the crypto market was at the peak of inflated expectations.**

The overly high expectations from Phase Two were not met, at least in the short term. What remained were many frustrated retail investors who only saw the quick buck. Many of them had also not invested in the technology and actually understood it, but only speculated on short-term profits. They were also the ones who had then bailed out again and turned their backs on the Bitcoin and Blockchain hype.

But some - the so-called hodlers - stayed on the ball, or rather on Bitcoin. And the cooling off has been good for the entire crypto ecosystem. It gave the serious developers time to work on their projects and most of the freeloaders left the stage again. The ensuing path of enlightenment has been built sustainably and makes way for real technological innovations.

Now, at least according to the Gartner hype cycle, it's time to slowly enter the plateau of productivity. This means that people are realizing the benefits of technology and it is slowly making its way into the mainstream. As of yet, it's impossible to estimate how long that will take. One thing is certain, however, at least from my point of view: staying on the ball is worthwhile.

If you follow the Gartner hype cycle, you can compare it with the development phase of the Internet. Analogously, we are currently in a development phase in which the technology is unfolding its great potential. Because with blockchain technology, too, we can assume that we are dealing with a technology that is here to stay.

There is much to suggest that blockchain technology, and Bitcoin as well, is at the beginning of a great development.

Conclusion on Blockchain Technology

The advantages that blockchain technology brings are obvious. It is a technology that can revolutionize diverse areas of life. Whether it is the energy sector, logistics or healthcare: blockchain can make processes more efficient and save resources.

Bitcoin is the best example of the technology's possibilities. As the most well-known application of blockchain technology, namely in the financial sector, it is already evident that Bitcoin can offer a real alternative to the current monetary system.

By looking at the Gartner hype cycle, we can surmise that we are at the beginning of a development that no one should miss. Perhaps we are looking at a unique opportunity that will bring us similar upheavals as the Internet.

But "Bitcoin's little brother" Ethereum also promises great things. Time to take a look at it in the next chapter.

6. Ethereum and Other Crypto Projects

Ethereum is considered by many crypto followers to be the project with the greatest potential next to Bitcoin. If the oldest of all cryptocurrencies is often referred to as the "digital gold", Ethereum is considered the "digital silver" - the second most precious and second most valuable among digital coins.

> **Ethereum is the second largest cryptocurrency by market capitalization. The Ethereum platform enables "smart contracts" that automate digital processes.**

But what makes Ethereum so special? First of all, the project of inventor Vitalik Buterin brings a new application form to the blockchain world, the so-called "smart contracts".

These "smart contracts" make it possible to automate digital processes and promise a host of cost savings for industry. But the plan to counter Bitcoin's energy-intensive "proof of work" process with a new system is also promising. But the project with the second largest market capitalization after Bitcoin has many more aces up its sleeve. Let's take a look at them!

Vitalik Buterin - Another Blockchain Genius

Vitalik Buterin is one of the most well-known minds in the world of cryptocurrencies. At the age of 19, he already published his white paper on Ethereum, a blockchain project that would quickly rise to become the second largest cryptocurrency ever.

However, he did not intend to copy Bitcoin with it. Rather, his white paper provided the idea for a project that would take the benefits of blockchain technology to a new level. Smart contracts were born!

Let's start a little earlier in the career of this boy wonder. Born on January 31, 1994, in the Russian city of Kolomna, he would embark on his first big journey at just six years old. His parents decided to emigrate to Canada in search of better paid work. Little did they know that their son would become a billionaire a few years later!

It soon became apparent that he was destined for great things. As early as the third grade, he was accepted into a gifted program. He soon became fascinated by numbers, mathematics and economics. To those around him, this seemed a bit disconcerting. The little genius was looked at askance from the side. His achievements, however, speak for themselves - at the age of 17, he received the bronze medal at the International Olympiad in Computer Science. It was not to be the last award.

Vitalik heard about Bitcoin at the age of 17, his father had told him about it. However, he didn't pay much attention to the project until 2013, when he kept hearing about blockchain technology at developer conferences. After Buterin published his white paper, he soon received an offer he couldn't refuse. With a grant of 100,000 Euros from the Thiel Fellowship, he got the opportunity to carry out his project.

Together with Mihai Alisie, Anthony Di Iorio, Charles Hoskinson, Joe Lubin and Gavin Wood, he tinkered with the Ethereum platform from then on. To continue funding the project, money was needed. So the team decided to release the cryptocurrency that was part of their project to the public: The first sale of Ether (ETH) to the public. And they succeeded. They collected a total of 31,000 Bitcoin, worth about $18 million at the time. Enough to get off the ground.

And it was to become one of the most successful projects to date alongside Bitcoin. While the price of an Ether was still at 0.75 cents in August 2015, it was to be worth just under 1,400 US dollars by January 2018. However, there is much more behind Ethereum than good rates. The technology is so sophisticated that the University of Basel was to award Vitalik Buterin an honorary doctorate in 2018. He was 24 years old at the time!

What is Ethereum?

Ethereum, like Bitcoin, is a blockchain. This means that it is a decentralized network that has no intermediary entities. Like Bitcoin, Ethereum does not require a bank or a state, but is built on technology alone.

The Ethereum platform offers people the opportunity to pay each other for services and the like. It provides the cryptocurrency Ether (ETH) for this purpose.

> **Ethereum is a blockchain that uses the cryptocurrency Ether (ETH).**

However, unlike Bitcoin, Ethereum is not a pure platform for currencies. In principle, it provides an update to Bitcoin. Because on Ethereum there is the possibility to run decentralized applications, so-called dApps. These can be thought of as similar to computer programs (apps), except that they do not require a central server. In addition, they consist of another ingenious innovation that Ethereum brings: smart contracts.

Smart Contracts and their application

Smart contracts can be programmed to be executed automatically. You design them to be told "do XY when Z happens."

Understanding this is easier than it may sound at first. You, too, have entered into a contract at one time or another, as probably a large percentage of the world's adult population has. And contracts always have certain conditions attached to claims. They can look like this:

"If you remit rent to me (Z), you may live in my apartment (XY)."

"If you borrow money from us (Z), you must pay interest on it (XY)."

"If you don't come to work regularly (Z), we'll kick them out (XY)."

We are talking about "if-then conditions" here. If something specific happens or is performed, then something happens or then they get something.

With smart contracts, we can put these if-then conditions into a computer program. They are then triggered automatically whenever something specific happens.

> **Smart contracts are automatic contracts that digitally map if-then conditions.**

This can save a lot of time and money. This is because there is no need for middlemen such as notaries. When you use smart contracts, you no longer need "middlemen" to execute the contracts. That's all done by the technology.

Proof of Stake

As part of a large-scale update, the Ethereum team is currently planning to change the consensus mechanism from "Proof of Work" to "Proof of Stake." The platform should benefit from this, as a lot of energy should be saved afterwards.

We remember: Bitcoin relies on the proof-of-work method. In short, this means that miners have to provide proof of work in order to claim the valid blockchain version.

In the proof-of-stake process, on the other hand, those participants who have a relatively large share of assets ("stake") in the network are given an opportunity to provide the latest blockchain version. You can think of it somewhat like a public company. Those who own a larger stake in the company also receive more voting rights.

Proof of Stake is an alternative consensus mechanism. It requires less power than Proof of Work. Those who have more tokens get more power in the network.

However, the participant who is subsequently allowed to pin the next block to the blockchain is randomly selected by the network. The more tokens one accumulates, the higher the chance of being randomly selected. As a participant who has been selected, you later receive a reward - the so-called "block subsidy".

We can think of it as something like a raffle. Whoever buys the most tickets has the highest probability of winning the prize. However, there is no guarantee that your lucky number will be drawn.

This mechanism therefore makes it possible to actively participate in the consensus mechanism simply by holding tokens. So you can help keep the network secure without having to do a lot of computing, as with Bitcoin.

Initial Coin Offerings - New Coins at the Push of a Button

Initial Coin Offerings - ICOs for short - offer a way to raise a lot of money for new crypto projects in a short period of time. Especially in the big crypto hype wave in 2017, it attracted many people to the crypto market. There were some new projects with substance, but most of the people were unfortunately freeloaders.

After all, with a bit of technical know-how, anyone can theoretically set up a new coin.

The technological basis is often the Ethereum blockchain. Anyone who wants to launch a new project issues a certain amount of new coins or "tokens". These are also called ERC-20 tokens, provided they are based on the Ethereum blockchain.

Investors can buy the new token, and the people behind the project get the money for it. In return, the tokens in the new network securitize certain functions. In most cases, this is a payment function. Anyone who buys new tokens is promised that they can do something with them in the new network, such as pay.

> **In an Initial Coin Offering (ICO), tokens are issued to fund a new crypto project.**

Of course, investors often hope that the project will gain more publicity, other people will join the project and, as a result, the price for the respective tokens will rise. This also makes it possible to profit on a speculative level - regardless of whether the project itself works at all or not.

In fact, Ethereum itself was also such a token project. In order to finance the development of its own platform, the team around Vitalik Buterin issued a new token - the Ether (ETH) - and collected Bitcoin for it.

In principle, you can imagine such a token sale similar to an IPO at a company. The big difference, however, is that the crypto market is largely unregulated. This means that there is no authority that monitors the new projects.

At the end of the day, this is a double-edged sword. Because on the one hand, it gives everyone the opportunity to collect capital. No matter what country they live in, whether they have a bank account, whether they have assets or not - with basic technical knowledge, anyone can launch their own coin!

The flip side of the coin is that there is also no one to police the 'Wild West' of cryptocurrencies. This also means that many crypto projects are shacks that have no substance. This makes it all the more important to inform yourself carefully and not to fall for every new coin just because it has a great description.

Thus, everyone who invests in a project must be aware that it is always possible to lose their entire capital. On the other hand, 100-fold increases are also possible within a very short time!

Among other things, it was the hope of spectacular profits that contributed to a large extent to the fact that the entire market overheated in 2017. Many sensed the chance to collect a lot of capital quickly through ICOs and threw new tokens onto the market like crazy.

Many people invested just as wildly and bought any coin they wanted. Anyone who read the previous chapter knows what happened next. An investment bubble formed because the expectations for the new technology were completely overblown. There were too many projects with too little substance and too much capital that was invested blindly. At the end of the year, the bubble burst and many new investors sold in panic. As a result, prices plummeted and the wheat separated from the chaff.

Decentralized Finance (DeFi)

Decentralized Finance - DeFi for short - is first of all the collective term for all decentralized financial services. A broad term, therefore, which at first glance includes the entire crypto market. Above all, the term sets itself apart from the traditional financial market. This is because the addition of "decentralized" means that it refers exclusively to financial services that do not require an intermediary. In the traditional sector, these include banks, stock exchanges and insurance companies. In the DeFi sector, all the tasks that are otherwise performed by such intermediaries are taken over by the protocol or technology.

The world of decentralized financial services is more promising than ever. In a society in which monopolies and oligarchs are increasingly losing people's trust, alternative services are needed. Instead of financial institutions, decentralized finance mostly relies on smart contracts.

The field of decentralized finance, which includes Bitcoin, does not need intermediaries such as banks or exchanges.

A well-known DeFi application is stable coins. These each represent the equivalent value of fiat currencies in the form of tokens. One unit of the stable coin USDT ("tether") is always worth one US dollar.

In the decentralized financial sector, stable coins serve the purpose of allowing cryptocurrencies to be exchanged for conventional currencies at any time. Going this route via stable coins saves time and money; after all, you don't have to exchange your money at a bank but can stay directly in the cryptoversum.

Non Fungible Token (NFT)

Non fungible tokens - NFT for short - are tokens that cannot be exchanged. Each NFT promises to be unique. Bitcoin, for example, is not one of the NFTs. Because each unit of the cryptocurrency is interchangeable, they all have the same function and value, Bitcoin is fungible.

If a token is non-fungible, on the other hand, it represents a unique asset. Thus, it cannot be exchanged one-to-one for another. Non-fungible tokens are, for example, works of art that have been digitized. For example, if you own a Banksy NFT, you own a unique digital share in one of the artworks. When the NFT is purchased, that ownership is securitized.

Each Non Fungible Token is unique and not exchangeable.

But in theory, all assets can be digitized through NFTs, whether pieces of music, artwork, or even possessions. The innovative thing about NFTs is that they are based on blockchain technology. Through this connection, one can always flawlessly establish and ensure that the respective token is also unique and genuine. Unlike conventional art objects, you never have to wonder whether you have just been taken in by a fake or whether you own the original. Since blockchains can also be viewed publicly, ownership is always well documented.

Security Token Offerings (STOs)

A Security Token Offering (STO) is an event in which digital securities are issued. However, unlike traditional token offerings, such events take place under the supervision of the respective authorities - they are regulated.

Those who participate in an STO on the buy side acquire one or more security tokens. This gives investors rights, such as a share in profits or a share in the assets.

Security token offerings are becoming increasingly popular, especially in the real estate sector. Shares of real estate are brought in the form of tokens and these are then offered for sale. So-called "tokenization" thus offers the possibility of dividing even large, immovable assets such as real estate into smaller parts.

Conclusion to the First Part: On the Way to the Revolution

Now we have reached the end of the first part of this book. And we have already learned a few things. We now know how money works and how it has happened again and again in history that money has lost its value through scarcity, inflation and other shenanigans. What has run through the history of money has been the realization that the current monetary system lacks a trustworthy monetary anchor.

Whether through currency reforms, the failure of Bretton Woods, or war bonds, our financial system is broken. The world's monetary elites manipulate the monetary system at will, and individual citizens often watch helplessly as their money is drained from their pockets.

Whereas in the past there was still the gold anchor, which forced politicians as well as banks and states to a certain discipline, now all floodgates are open. There are no limits to money printing, the consequences are inflated real assets, real estate bubbles, stock bubbles and the general devaluation of money.

And then there is Bitcoin. A decentralized money or gold system that is completely independent of states. What's more, a limit on the money supply is set by code, and the supply is getting scarcer and scarcer. And there is much to suggest that it is not just the digital version of gold. It's even better than the "real" gold!

That's because Bitcoin cleverly solves the trust problem we face in the international financial system. Here, you no longer have to trust individual people or institutions. But only the technology and the inscribed computer code.

This computer code opposes the old and fragile system with something completely new. It's faster, cheaper, more reliable - I don't think it's presumptuous to call this a revolution!

Once again, here is an overview of Bitcoin's advantages:

Decentralized: Bitcoin does not need banks

Universal: Bitcoin does not need exchange offices

Infallible: Bitcoin does not need humans in its administration

Cannot be manipulated: the blockchain is transparent and cannot be changed

Secure: Bitcoin has no central points of attack, unlike centralized systems

Limited quantity and digital scarcity: the maximum quantity of 21 million Bitcoin prevents money from being created without hindrance

Comparable to the Internet, which provides information to everyone worldwide, Bitcoin can provide access to money to everyone worldwide. The addition of Ethereum and Smart Contracts completes the revolution - after all, it offers the opportunity to create entire business sectors from scratch.

I was convinced by this system. For me, Bitcoin is far superior to fiat money, i.e. Euros, US dollars and the like! I am sure that it is a unique opportunity to take the fate over the finances into one's own hands. It is now a matter of being there when this technological revolution develops in a similar way as the Internet did back then.

But of course, the same applies here: Is there a guarantee? No. Everyone acts on their own responsibility, and that applies especially to investments. Even I cannot give you a guarantee that Bitcoin will not fail in an unforeseen way.

But is it plausible that Bitcoin will prevail? Absolutely. I am convinced of it. Otherwise, I wouldn't have written this book.

If you are too, it is now time to take the next step. In the next chapter, we will look together at how to become a successful investor.

7. Bitcoin and Crypto Investments: The Big Opportunity

It cannot be stressed enough: You should never invest in financial products if you are not familiar with them. This is true not only for stocks or real estate, but especially for Bitcoin. After the first half of this book, you have already gathered important basic knowledge. We can probably say: you can approach the topic of a possible investment with a good feeling.

Nevertheless, you should take another critical look at yourself and weigh the opportunities and risks of this new and volatile asset class.

Here are a few important points:

- Are you convinced that Bitcoin or even Ethereum can solve problems and offer advantages over the current financial system?

- Are you aware that volatility brings big increases, but also deep drops, and therefore time horizon (the further the better) plays a crucial role?

- Know this: Revolutions have winners - maybe you and me - but also losers. And these losers, consisting of states, banks and financial service providers, are powerful and will try to defend their sinecures. With all means!

- Is an inflation-proof investment important to you?

- Do you believe that the Bitcoin and Ethereum networks could follow similar developments as their predecessors Amazon, Google, Facebook and Co.

Should you consider a majority of these points plausible and likely, then an investment probably makes a lot of sense for you.

Speculation or Investment?

Any investment that aims to make you money in the future is a form of speculation. After all, no one can predict the future! Certain developments are probable or even likely, but no one can say for sure what will happen.

But what makes a speculation a serious investment? It only becomes one when it is paired with a lot of knowledge about the matter as well as a responsible commitment and time flexibility.

To give you a little insight: I myself started with five percent of my total investment capital and have increased it to 30 percent over time. The crazy thing is that by now - despite temporary crashes - the value of my crypto investments exceeds the rest of my portfolio by four times. So that you too can profit from this market and make good decisions, I have compiled the most important insights and experiences below.

Investment 1x1

There are a few things that are essential to keep in mind when investing. If you take them to heart, you are on the comparatively safe side.

Only invest what you can handle.

There's no question that the outlook is good. As you will know after reading this book, there is a good chance that both Bitcoin and blockchain technology will succeed in the future. However, no one, neither you nor I, can predict the future. That's why the basic rule applies:

Only invest as much as you are willing to lose to the maximum!

Because if you put your savings or retirement savings at risk, you won't sleep well. Even worse: take out a loan in order to invest with it. This is definitely not advisable.

Emotions are a bad advisor

If you get carried away by your emotions, you will most likely not be a good investor. The main distinction here is between two extremes: FUD and FOMO.

"FUD" is an acronym and consists of the English words "Fear, Uncertainty and Doubt". Those who get carried away by bad news, for example, may sell out of panic at a bad price. And are all the more annoyed when the price rises again.

"FOMO" stands for "Fear of Missing Out". Here we are dealing with the counterpart to FUD. If you want to jump on the bandwagon in a hurry because prices are just about to explode, you may be buying at the wrong moment.

This makes it all the more important to take a deep look inside oneself before making investment decisions and ask oneself: Am I acting in carefully deliberate and rational manner right now? Or am I letting myself be carried away by my emotions, perhaps even by greed? If this is the case, you should rather take a step back and wait until the situation has eased. Tomorrow is another day!

Realize Profits

Realize: one Bitcoin will always be worth one Bitcoin, no matter how high or low the exchange rate is.

This means: you have only made a profit or a loss when you realize it, i.e. when you exchange your BTC back into Euros. If you have reached a certain investment goal, don't be afraid to realize it. If you make a profit, you didn't sell too early!

Make a plan and stick to it

In order not to get carried away by your emotions, it is incredibly important to have a firm plan.

Sit down calmly once and answer the following questions:

1. What is my investment horizon? (1 year, 5 years, 10 years?)

2. Is there a price at which I want to skim profits? If yes, what is the price? How high are the profits you want to skim?

3. Is there a minimum price at which I want to exit, because otherwise I will be afraid of losing too much money? If so, how low is it?

4. What is my daily, monthly and annual budget?

5. How can I tell that my emotions are running away with me right now?

Once you have answered these questions for yourself, you have a plan. Stick to that plan and don't get sidetracked!

Invest in Batches

Experts who have been in bitcoin investing for a while recommend: Don't invest all at once! This applies to both buying and selling. Those who stick to their plan should buy and sell in batches. For example, at regular intervals, always 25 percent of the intended capital. This minimizes the risk of buying or selling at a particularly unfavorable price and then getting angry when the price is even better.

Anticyclical Investing
Buy when the guns are thundering, sell, when the violins are playing.

Anticyclical investing is something for advanced investors. They keep a close eye on the market and try to react in time. When prices have just fallen, you strike - for example, during a crash or economic crisis. Then the entry opportunities are often particularly favorable and the upside potential is relatively high. So you buy when the cannons are thundering.

On the other hand, with an anticyclical investment, it is important to realize profits when prices are particularly high. For example, when the Bitcoin price has again reached a new all-time high - then it can be worthwhile to deduct part of your profits and hope for lower entry prices.

However, anti-cyclical investing requires not only a good feel for the market, but also a fair amount of luck. Very few manage to "time" the market.

Cost-Dollar-Average: The Bitcoin Savings Plan

A popular method to invest in Bitcoin is called "Cost-Dollar-Average". This is a type of savings plan. You invest a certain amount at a set time each month and buy bitcoin from it.

It might look like this: You set an amount you can handle each month without it hurting you - whether that's 20, 50, 100 or 1,000 euros, you know best. Then you set a fixed time - either weekly, fortnightly or even monthly and always buy bitcoin at that time.

This option will even out the fluctuations in the exchange rate. You may sometimes invest at a higher rate and sometimes at a lower rate. But your average rate will in all likelihood adjust so that you come out with a profit in the long run.

> **Cost-Dollar Average is considered a good way to even out price fluctuations over the long term.**

The best thing about it is that you don't have to constantly monitor the rates and go crazy when the bitcoin rate has gone up or down. You can sit back, relax, and watch your Bitcoin wealth grow bigger.

There are also online providers that offer such savings plans. To do this, you simply set up a standing order that regularly deducts the money from your account. Providers include www.bitpanda.com or getbittr.com.

Bitcoin Cycles: a Guarantee for Price?

The number of new Bitcoins coming into circulation is constantly decreasing. This, as we already know, is fixed in the code. For each new "mined" block, the miners receive a fixed reward. Currently, that's 6.25 BTC plus the transaction fees.

Halving

But this reward is halved every 210,000 blocks - usually lasting about four years. This event is called "halving."

> **Halving is when Bitcoin's supply replenishment is cut in half. As a result, Bitcoin becomes more scarce over time.**

This regular halving ensures that the supply of new Bitcoins steadily decreases. And that ends up having an impact on the Bitcoin price. In the past, the Bitcoin price has always risen in the wake of halvings. The first halving took place in November 2012, and the reward for miners was halved from 50 to 25 BTC per block. Subsequently, the price rose from $12 to nearly $1,150 within a year.

The second halving had an even more impressive impact.

At the time of the second halving, which took place in July 2016, the price rose from US$650 to nearly US$20,000 in December

2017, halving the supply supply of digital gold from 25 to 12.5 BTC per block.

Then, in May 2020, the third halving occurred. The reward was tightened from 12.5 BTC to 6.25 BTC. The bitcoin price subsequently rose from US$8,700 at the time of the halving to just under US$63,000 in April 2021.

The next halving is expected to take place on March 12, 2024 at 17:24. We can be curious to see how the price will develop until then.

Cycle Theory: the Stock-to-Flow Model

Based on the halving, Bitcoin's valuation can be divided into four-year cycles. Among Bitcoiners, one model in particular enjoys great popularity is the stock-to-flow model.

It is used to evaluate the rarity of an asset based on various data. It puts the distribution of a commodity - in this case Bitcoins - in relation to the number of new distributions in a given period.

And that's where Bitcoin does very well: bitcoin is being used more and more, while less and less of it is being produced. Using past prices, the stock-to-flow model therefore predicts a price of $288,000 by the end of 2024.

History does not repeat itself...

...but it does rhyme. In other words, just because the bitcoin price has followed the stock-to-flow model in the past (or is it more the other way around?), there is no guarantee that it will do so in the future. But it is not unlikely.

That is also the crux of share price forecasts: no one, really no one, can say with certainty whether they will come true. No one has yet found the right crystal ball. Price forecasts and models are always only approximations of reality.

Crypto Lending: Interest on Cryptocurrencies

People who have some money "on the high side" or even savings, sooner or later face the question of what to do with this money. But the banks hardly offer any more incentives here. Interest rates are so low in some cases that they are barely enough to cushion the inflation rate. Those who accumulate larger amounts of money can even be penalized. The punitive interest rates that some banks charge for holding money seem absurd in some cases. That's why the question of what to do with their money instead of letting it sit in the bank is relatively urgent for many people.

The world of cryptocurrencies offers a solution for this as well: crypto-lending. For those who already own Bitcoins or other cryptocurrencies have the opportunity to "make their money work for them." Certain platforms offer investors the opportunity to lend their cryptocurrencies ("lending"). When other people borrow these cryptocurrencies ("borrowing"), they get paid interest.

> **With crypto lending, you can lend your cryptocurrencies and get paid interest.**

Anyone who has gotten to know the crypto world a bit will be able to guess: The clocks also tick a bit differently when it comes to money lending. Anyone who wants to borrow money in the area of cryptocurrencies, for example, does not have to deposit a Schufa report and prove their creditworthiness. Rather, the person simply deposits a certain amount of a cryptocurrency (e.g. Bitcoin) and receives fiat money (e.g. euros) in return. The deposited Bitcoins are later referred to as "collateral".

So if you want to get money in the short term but don't want to sell your Coins, Lending is a good way to get money. This is, especially for long-term investors or so-called "Hodlers", a great way to become "liquid". This way, they can continue to hold their Bitcoin and have fiat money at the same time.

Those who make their cryptocurrencies available on the other side can also benefit from this new type of finance. Those who make their money available with a crypto lending provider are rewarded with high interest rates. These range - depending on the provider - between 4 and 12 percent.

But, as you might have guessed, higher interest rates also mean higher risk. The industry is still in its infancy, for example, which is why technical problems or failures can occur. Also, you are not always protected against possible insolvencies of the providers. To be fair, the technology is still young and growing. That's why you always have to check exactly which provider you're dealing with.

By the way, most lending platforms automatically assign lenders and borrowers. In the process, they determine who is the best fit for each other.

Staking

Another way to make your money work for you in the field of cryptocurrencies is "staking". For this, you make your coins available to support the proof-of-stake mechanism of certain cryptocurrencies. In simple terms, staking means that coins are logged in for a certain time and cannot be used by the owner. In return, he or she receives a reward.

We remember: in the proof-of-stake process, the network randomly selects the participant who gets to create the next valid block. This participant also receives a reward. Those who own a high number of tokens ("Stake") increase their chances of being drawn from the lottery pot.

There are different ways to do this. Either you perform the staking directly via your own wallet or you use one of the many crypto exchanges that support you. The advantage of staking is that you can actively participate in the network without having to provide large computing power from computers, as is the case with Bitcoin. You do not have to buy any hardware, but simply invest in the respective coin with which Staking is possible.

These include the projects Cardano (ADA), Algorand (ALGO), Tezos (XTZ), Celo (CELO) and Mina (MINA).

If you want to increase your chances of being drawn from the lottery pot, you can also look for so-called staking pools. In such pools, several participants throw their tokens together to increase their chances of winning. The reward is also shared later, of course.

Staking pools increase the chances of getting rewards.

The downside to such staking pools is that providers often charge higher fees. You could also say that the entrance fee to swim in the pool is quite high. This is again due to the fact that the administrative effort for such a pool is quite high. Once again, it becomes clear that as soon as an intermediary comes into play, the matter becomes more costly.

What is the Bitcoin worth?

First, the question of Bitcoin's value can be explained at a very basic level. A Bitcoin is always worth as much as someone is willing to pay for it. The basic law of supply and demand applies to Bitcoin as it does to any other economic good. If many people want a certain good (demand) but there is only a certain amount (supply) of it, the price will also rise. On the other hand, if there is a large supply but a decreasing demand, the price decreases. But how do you determine what price is fair?

The value of Bitcoin is calculated from the interaction of supply and demand.

Critics of Bitcoin repeatedly say that Bitcoin has no intrinsic value. This metric, also known as "intrinsic value," is generally difficult to measure. According to Gabler's banking encyclopedia, it initially describes the value of an object to be determined as "substance, yield or other substantive characteristics." So far, so unclear.

To think about the value of Bitcoin, one must first be aware of what Bitcoin actually offers. Bitcoin, we now know, stands for a monetary system that has no barriers. An alternative currency that is counterfeit-proof and cannot be manipulated. Isn't that already an intrinsic value? This is certainly debatable.

The value of a Bitcoin is ultimately also fed by what it promises: a way out of the current monetary system. This is characterized by inflation and by the uncontrolled distribution of money by central banks.

Ultimately, the value of Bitcoin lies in its function as a store of value. Because, we remember, Bitcoin is a scarce commodity - even a very scarce one. The new gold money is becoming increasingly scarce and thus increasingly valuable. Chances are good that this development will continue for a long time.

The maximum quantity of 21 million protects Bitcoin from inflation.

The problem with Bitcoin, however, is its high price fluctuations. In today's market environment, it is nothing unusual for the Bitcoin price to fluctuate by several thousand euros within a few weeks.

However, according to previous findings, this is mainly due to the fact that we are still dealing with such a young asset. In the long run, the price will probably stabilize. Because the more participants find their way onto the market, the more stable the prices will become.

> **The more participants find their way to the crypto markets, the more likely stable prices will become.**

For brave investors, bitcoin certainly offers a good option already today. According to various price models and assessments, the chances are good that Bitcoin will establish itself as an alternative store of value. More and more companies, especially from the US, are already daring to integrate Bitcoin into their portfolios. These include Tesla around crypto figurehead Elon Musk and the payment service provider PayPal. For them, the question of Bitcoin's intrinsic value hardly seems to arise. How does it look to you?

Speculative Bubbles in the Crypto Market

Speculative bubbles are, generally speaking, market situations in which the prices of goods exceed their actual value many times over. Due to a heated mood, such as hype, many people smell a good deal and are willing to pay high prices for a certain good.

The best example of a speculative bubble is the tulip mania in the first half of the 17th century in the Netherlands. Tulips were an object of admiration - the rich and beautiful liked to decorate their gardens with the handsome flowers. But gradually tulip bulbs became rarer, after all, there were only a limited number on the market. This, in turn, caused prices to rise. The basic principle of supply and demand drove the price up.

Business-minded people sensed their opportunity. More and more people wanted to get into the tulip business and sell their bulbs for a little more money than the price they had originally paid. As a result, by the 1630s even the lowest classes of the population were involved in the tulip trade. Prices eventually rose so much due to high demand that no one was willing to pay them anymore. The market for tulips collapsed in 1937, with many people now facing piles of wilted, worthless tulips and rotten tulip bulbs.... Greed had driven them to invest in something they knew nothing about.

Speculative bubbles are driven by people's greed and, through blind investments, cause the prices of certain goods to inflate.

As a result, there have been speculative bubbles throughout human history, such as the South Sea Bubble (1720), the dot-com bubble (2000), and the U.S. housing bubble (2007), among many others. When there is hype around a particular topic - whether it's real estate or tulips - people speculate that prices will rise. This then leads to everyone wanting their piece of the pie.

But what about the crypto market? Here, too, we are always running the risk of the market inflating artificially. We know from the previous chapter, for example, that new technologies are always accompanied by exaggerated expectations. As a result, prices rise, even if they may not be justified. Especially in the crypto sector, there are always a lot of free riders who try to profit from the big hype.

The Bitcoin price was completely overheated in 2017. News of crypto millionaires who had increased their capital within a very short time circulated in the media. In some cases, the network itself could not keep up at all. The Bitcoin network was in part so overloaded that transactions in the blockchain were stuck for several days. Transaction fees also rose to unprecedented heights.

This makes it all the more important to take a close look at the issue. For example, it is worth talking to experts, reading magazines from the scene and always informing yourself about different sources. This is the only way to get a feel for whether the markets are currently overheated or not.

According to Robert Shiller, a US economist and professor at Yale University, you can tell if a market is in a bubble by the following signs:

- Sharp rise in prices

- Unbelievable stories about why prices are rising

- A large number of people reporting that they have made a lot of money

- "FOMO" - people reporting that they are upset that they haven't invested yet

- Increased media coverage

So once again, when the bitcoin price spikes upwards by double-digit percentages in a very short period of time, you might want to think again before investing. It helps to read through the relevant news portals and look for reasons for this.

Are there perhaps large companies that have announced an integration of cryptocurrencies? Or is there even a state that has officially recognized bitcoin as a means of payment? Such fundamental news can be signs that price increases are justified. If it becomes difficult to find comprehensible reasons, it may well be that the market is overheated.

But here, too, caution is advised: markets are unpredictable. Even if price increases seem justified, it may be that they will drop again.

This is because mixed forms are also possible. For example, a justified price increase can also be followed by a phase of hype and overheating, and vice versa.

Conclusion

If you have understood and internalized the advice in this chapter, you have an important basic knowledge that unsuccessful investors do not have: You are informed. After all, information is one of the most important, if not the most important, prerequisite for putting your money to good use and growing it.

But here's another important tip I'd like to repeat at this point: start small. Take a small amount, invest it, and watch yourself do well with it.

Start your investment with small amounts.

If you have the time, quietly immerse yourself in the Bitcoin and blockchain space, get informed and stay on the ball - for example, by keeping a close eye on current developments in the blockchain space and getting a feel for the matter based on new developments.

8. Financial Freedom

Getting started: What you need

To be able to buy Bitcoin yourself, the very first thing you need is a digital wallet, also called a "wallet". This wallet is where the bitcoin will be stored afterwards.

Each of these wallets has a public address, the public key. This address consists of a 34-digit composition of numbers and letters. It is the "Bitcoin account number".

Example of a Bitcoin address:
12c6DSiU4Rq3P4ZxziKxzrL5LmMBrzjrJX

Now how do you get such an address? First of all, that depends on what kind of wallet you use. Most wallets create the addresses by themselves, so all you have to do is copy them later.

Online wallet: The "Hot" Variant

If you want to get started with Bitcoins quickly, you can opt for a so-called "hot wallet". It is constantly connected to the Internet and is therefore referred to as "hot".

To do this, you sign up for one of the numerous crypto exchanges, for example, open an account and you can buy your coins online. Another option is to set up hot wallets on an app and then use it to send and receive Bitcoin.

The downside to hot wallets is that they are always online. Therefore, in most cases, they are connected to the respective exchanges or brokers. And these are unfortunately not as secure as the blockchain itself. That is why it can happen that they are hacked. Digital burglars could steal the Bitcoins as a result, which has happened again and again in the past. Therefore, a "cold wallet" is recommended.

Cold Wallet: The Secure Variant

So-called cold or hardware wallets look something like a USB stick and function in a similar way. If you buy such a wallet, it is delivered to your home and you then have to connect it to your computer. With an appropriate program, you can then store the Bitcoins on your stick and keep it in a safe place. It is also secured with a special password that only you know!

Cold wallets are considered the safest way to store your coins.

So, if you want to buy Bitcoin the safe way, it is best to sign up with an exchange where you can buy Bitcoin directly. Once the Bitcoins have been purchased there then, you send them to your cold wallet and voila! The digital coins are safe.

For Professionals: Paper Wallet

If you want something more complicated, you can also create a "paper wallet". To do this, log on to www.blockchain.com and create a Bitcoin address. Write it down on a piece of paper and store it in a safe place. Preferably, inside a safe. However, be careful: If you lose the piece of paper, you also lose your coins!

However, by writing down your data on a piece of paper and storing it in a safe, for example, you can also increase the security of a cold wallet. If one should lose this nevertheless, one has so an additional protection.

9. Risks and Opportunities

Revolutions are social upheavals. They always bring great opportunities – but, of course, there is always a risk involved. So too with Bitcoin - be it the thing itself, the uncertain timeline, or the risk of political "killer laws" that might try to preserve the dominance of the political and financial elite.

That's why, especially if you're toying with the idea of investing money, you should weigh the pros and cons thoughtfully.

For your orientation, I will still give a forecast below where the Bitcoin's journey will take us - including a short-, medium- and long-term price forecast.

What is even more important, however, is the developments and changes that digital gold will bring to the economy and society. This is because the question still remains, whether Satoshi Nakamoto's vision will prevail. Will Bitcoin make it possible in the long run to give people more financial freedom from banks and third parties? Or will it, after all, become a new asset class that, like so much else, will be dominated by today's financial elite and used for their enrichment?

The Bitcoin Ban

As much as Bitcoin promises, even this ingenious concept cannot be perfect and cannot protect itself from all dangers.

Especially powerful players such as the US Securities and Exchange Commission (SEC for short) are a thorn in the side of the cryptocurrency. The Chinese government is also not exactly positive about cryptocurrencies - its promises of more autonomy for the people are too promising. And here we also come to one of the risks: A Bitcoin ban could make access to the digital currency much more difficult. Such efforts have also had a negative impact time and again on the price in the past. But can Bitcoin be banned at all?

The short answer is no! The long one: the blockchain runs without interruption, without a state and without a bank. And you can't ban a decentralized network just like that. However, states can ban trading on it, as China has already tried. Also, intervention by regulators, such as imposing high taxes, can have a significant impact on Bitcoin.

> **A general ban on Bitcoin is not enforceable. However, it is possible to ban trading in it, which can lead to severe restrictions.**

Interventions of a governmental and regulatory nature can influence Bitcoin and thus its price development, at least in the short term. In the long run, however, I believe that the power of decentralization will prevail.

Energy Consumption and Environmental Awareness

For many people, the high power consumption that Bitcoin incurs to ensure the security of the network is not justified. At a time when everyone has to face the question of their own CO2 emissions, the energy issue does not cast Bitcoin in a good light. However, as we already know from Chapter 3, there are ways and means to face this problem.

Ultimately, all people who use Bitcoin have it in their own hands to ensure an appropriate balance. Miners will also have to face this problem sooner or later.

I am optimistic that Bitcoin and especially its large community will also solve this problem for themselves.

Quantum Computers

Time and again, the rumor is circulating through the crypto kitchen that quantum computers would theoretically be able to crack the blockchain. According to current forecasts, these should be ready for use as early as 2026 and then be able to crack even the bombproof blockchain technology within a short period of time.

It must be conceded here that this danger is real and one must follow developments in this area with a watchful eye. But these developments are, of course, well known in the blockchain and Bitcoin community. It is primarily up to the developers around the blockchain to prepare the technology for these dangers.

However, there is also an opportunity here for potential investors: those who keep an eye on the market and regularly inform themselves on relevant portals can react in time if dangers should arise. The "next big thing" could be a blockchain project that comes along with a quantum-safe blockchain. Or one that upgrades the security system accordingly.

Volatility

The sometimes high price fluctuations are another aspect that makes many people shy away from investing in Bitcoin. If you are unlucky enough to invest at the time of the all-time high, your virtual assets - at least in Euros - may shrink by up to 80 percent within a few weeks or months.

In such cases, it pays to have staying power. Because the rule still applies: losses are only made by those who realize them. A Bitcoin will always be worth a Bitcoin, even if its price fluctuates in Euros or US dollars.

However, those who do not let themselves be upset by short-term price fluctuations have been rewarded in the past. Because the all-time high of the old cycle was often in the area of the bottom of the new cycle.

So is high volatility a real risk for investors? In my opinion, the answer is no. If, as I strongly suspect, Bitcoin establishes itself as the new, digital gold anchor in the long run, it will hardly matter whether the price falls or rises within a few weeks or months.

Crypto Competition

Bitcoin is – as we know it - the largest and oldest of all cryptocurrencies. But will "mother bitcoin" also sit on the throne of cryptocurrencies for all times? The answer is: we don't know. It can always happen that a new coin comes along that is better, faster, more environmentally friendly and more efficient. So it can also happen that this new coin will eventually knock Bitcoin off its throne and become the "next big thing." Even in the development of the Internet with all its companies, there have been pioneers over time, who have been overtaken by better systems.

Yet, it is likely, in my estimation, that Bitcoin will not lose any of its charisma anytime soon. As before, the cryptocurrency is sitting firmly in the saddle - with a market capitalization of over $800 billion, it already has Facebook and Tesla in its pocket.

I can't give you a guarantee, of course. But I don't think the status quo will change much in the near future.

No Government and Institutional Oversight

The genius of Bitcoin is that you can't monitor it - no government, no bank has any influence on how the cryptocurrency develops and who handles it. You only become visible as soon as you get back into the "fiat money" area, i.e. buying or selling Bitcoins on an exchange against Euros or Dollars. This is because all users have to register there with their full name and address in accordance with the "Know Your Customer" guidelines.

Apart from that, however, the decentralized money system eludes government intervention. The technology and the computer code itself cannot be manipulated. Finally, this also means that every person who puts Bitcoin in their digital wallet is responsible for their own coins. Among Bitcoiners, they also say "Not your keys, not your coins!". So if you forget or misplace your private keys, you have no way to recover them. This is because there is no "forgot password" button on the blockchain.

The impossibility of state and institutional monitoring is thus both an opportunity and a risk. On the one hand, no one has to submit to control of their money; on the other hand, everyone is therefore obliged to take care of their money themselves. For me, this aspect - which could also be described as financial emancipation - is a clear plus!

Inflation Protection and Reserve Currency
Let's move on to the opportunities that Bitcoin offers. Bitcoin offers a wonderful protection against inflation and the devaluation of fiat currencies such as the US dollar, Euro or Swiss franc. This is because Bitcoin, as should be clear after reading this book, is a decentralized digital currency with a maximum money supply of 21 million coins. The amount of coins cannot be artificially increased and, as digital gold, is the hedge against crisis-ridden currency.

And as such, the cryptocurrency could even become the world's reserve currency for central banks. Because, let's face it, what better hedge than an independent monetary system?

Once Bitcoin's advantages are recognized by the majority of people, banks and states will no longer be able to resist this realization. The first U.S. banks are already doing it and putting some Bitcoins in their digital vaults. In doing so, they are preparing the best ground for the mass adoption of the cryptocurrency.

And when this kicks in, everyone who got in early will be happy. So I'm sure Bitcoin has a bright future ahead of it.

Digital scarcity

Bitcoin brings something unique to the world: it manages to be the first commodity to create digital scarcity. Bitcoin is becoming more scarce and therefore more valuable. The redistribution of wealth that comes with it is in full swing. More and more people are jumping on the Bitcoin bandwagon and want to be there when this incorruptible gold anchor catches on.

The New Gold Anchor

Bitcoin can offer millions of people access to a monetary system - and to all those who have been excluded from it until now. With the ability to send money across borders in seconds, Bitcoin has the potential to leave the competition around Western Union, as well as other payment providers, miles behind it.

Moreover, Bitcoin now offers a unique opportunity to participate in the redistribution of wealth. I think it is very likely that Bitcoin will continue to gain acceptance. So financial participation in the next technological revolution is an opportunity to consider taking.

Why? Bitcoin is the new gold anchor. Bitcoin is even better than gold because the cryptocurrency is digital, predictable and bombproof.

All the opportunities we've revisited in this chapter boil down to one thing: Bitcoin's supply shortage and unbeatable scarcity make it highly likely that its price will continue to rise in the long run.

And even the risks that could potentially threaten Bitcoin have ultimately turned out to be opportunities. After all, all of them can be mastered in one way or another by the industrious developer community.

10. My Investments

Now, to conclude this book, I want to share with you some personal insights I have made as an investor and crypto beginner, but also as a private person. In this chapter, however, I will not only share my experiences. I will also reveal my price predictions and you will get an insight into my investment plan.

However, there is one thing I want to emphasize at this point: There can be no guarantee for my assessments. Really only invest, if you do so, of your own free will and have come to the conclusion yourself having found reasons for it. Everyone is responsible for his or her own money!

Of Greed and Steady Hands - What I Have Learned

My first encounter with Bitcoin was in 2017, and I've learned a lot since then. Let me tell you: some things went wrong. But a lot also went very well - that's how it is when you take the plunge and venture into uncharted territory. That's why I want to share my experiences with you. Because I hope and am sure that you could take some things with you for your first steps in this matter. But I do not only want to describe my successes, but also my mistakes. Because, as we all know, we learn learn from them best.

Phase 1 (mid-2017)

My son-in-law - a physicist with a PhD and an expert in risk management - was the first to tell me about Bitcoins and cryptocurrencies. It was mid-2017 when he had told me how exciting these new blockchain projects were. He also told me about Ether and that he had invested a small amount. My interest was aroused. Without further ado, I asked him to buy me some Ether as well.

He gave me an important lesson right away, which I then also followed: Always invest only as much as I could bear in the event of a total loss. He told me that the value of Ether could multiply significantly. But that also means - as always with investments - an increased risk!

Then he gave me another strategy: risk mitigation. This means that if the price were to increase about fivefold, I would sell Ether again for the same value of the capital invested. This way, I would have my stake back in and could watch more in a relaxed way how the price develops.

Phase 2 (end of 2017 - mid 2018)

My entry price in Ether was between $200 and $300. After some ups and downs, things got really exciting at the end of the year. The Bitcoin price exploded and reached its all-time high of just under 20,000 US dollars on December 17. And the Ether price also shot through the roof. Soon it should be at over 1,000 euros. As a crypto newbie, I didn't understand why or how, but found the whole thing all the more exciting. I looked at the prices at least 10 times a day and rode the "crypto roller coaster". What a journey!

I had not yet reached my goal - a five-fold increase in investment. So I continued to wait in anticipation. But then the crash came, the Bitcoin price sank in on itself, taking all the altcoins down with it. Ether, too, of course! After four months we were at about 400 US dollars and half a year later below 200 US dollars. That meant: loss instead of wealth!

Interim conclusion: This is what I learned from phase 1 and 2.

What a roller coaster ride! First I saw the big gains and suddenly everything crashed again. Even below my entry price. Then I quickly realized: I had invested the right amount. Because I didn't need the money, so I didn't have to worry too much. Thus, I had complied with investor rule number 1.

What else I learned: Never (!) invest in an area of which you don't have at least some basic knowledge. Furthermore, it was wrong to blindly copy a strategy. The reason being, the earlier in the stage of a price development one enters, the higher the price chances. Profits must be realized, otherwise they are not profits. In my case, a partial exit at 300 or 400 percent would have been more logical and goal-oriented.

Another mistake was to constantly follow the price. Especially in the field of cryptocurrencies, emotions boil over quickly. It is much more important to understand the underlying price drivers. It is important to ask yourself: are the current rises justified? Or is the market just boiling over? Only those who observe the market closely can make rational decisions!

Phase 3 (mid 2018 - mid 2019)

After I had digested the small shock from the first phases, I started to immerse myself in the matter. And the only way to do that is through information. I began to study cryptocurrencies and blockchain technology at seminars, such as from the Frankfurt School of Finance. I also found out about these new technologies in trade journals (BTC-ECHO) and through newsletters (Kraken, Coinbase, etc.). Inquisitively, I soaked it all up. In the process, I noticed several things. One of the most important things I learned was that with new markets, high volatility is perfectly normal. If a stock price is gaining several hundred percent, you can almost expect it to crash down 80 percent.

This was very similar in the early years of the big platform giants Amazon, Google and Microsoft. No question: if you have a good hand here, you can make a lot of money quickly with day trading. But if you lack the necessary bit of luck or have a restless hand, you can also quickly gamble away your money. That was clearly too hot for me.

So I decided to become a "Hodler": hold, buy and wait! Due to the similarity to shares, I am convinced that the safe way with Bitcoin is to think and act in the long term.

After all, in the long run, you usually profit. And the more I learned about Bitcoin, the more convinced I was: The price will rise again! Fortunately, I never had to sell out of necessity. That is the most important thing with all volatile investments, since losses are only made if you realize them!

Phase 4 (mid 2019 - mid 2021)

So now I was immersed in the material. It was clear to me: the next step can be taken. So I started a crypto fund at Iconomi. Since then, I actively manage a part of my cryptocurrencies and hold the larger part in good Hodler fashion.

The idea: still make increases during the sideways movement of the markets and be better than the market. Shouldn't be that hard with all the accumulated knowledge! At least that's what I thought.

And it turned out: yes, it is difficult! Anyone who knows how often "managed funds" by seemingly professional traders barely, or not at all, outperform the market in stocks, knows exactly what I mean.

I persisted and poked around the market. DeFi, NFT's and other projects - I got in and out and dove deeper: Learning by doing! But I soon had to admit to myself: My actively managed crypto holdings and fund did not perform one iota better than my hoarded crypto stocks.

At the time of writing (fall 2021), my Bitcoin, Ether and other cryptos are up. And again, I think: when the bitcoin price was still above 50,000 euros, the profit would have been even greater. Should I have sold some of it? Maybe next time.

Interim Conclusion: Learnings Phase 3 and 4

Accumulating knowledge was incredibly important to help me better navigate the market. Only in this way was I able to recognize that the fundamental laws of the financial world also apply in the realm of cryptocurrencies. First and foremost, those of supply and demand!

And this was confirmed: without knowing the basics and laws of the technology, one lacks confidence in a good future. Much like many people felt when the "new" tech companies like Amazon and Google crawled out of their garages and beckoned with new, unknown technologies. How can you have confidence in something you don't understand?

Another realization: you have to be a savvy professional to be better than the market. Little hustle, a completely steady hand, and a dose of luck to boot.

In addition, it was something deeply human that kept interfering with me: emotions! If the prices went up, greed set in, if the prices went down, fear set in. But only a little, because through my experience as an entrepreneur and consultant I know that products and projects with an important and beneficial added value for the target group will always be successful in the long run!

And of course, adhering to Investment Rule 1 has also given me peace of mind. Meanwhile I know: Fear and greed, both are bad advisors. Better is a future prognosis based on facts. This is also not a guarantee, but it gives a better feeling and you can always check if the assumptions are still about right as time goes on.

My Prediction: Bitcoin Quo Vadis?

There are a few factors that suggest the Bitcoin price will continue to rise in the future.

The *scarcity* of Bitcoin alone, as explained in detail in this book, argues that the price one pays for Bitcoin will continue to climb. The rash of reasons for this can be found in the basic rules of the market economy: supply and demand. If demand increases while supply remains the same, prices also rise. After all, the market itself evaluates what is good, reliable and stable value money - this is less in the power of interest-driven institutions such as central banks and governments. I am sure: Bitcoin will be able to hold its own against fiat money. At some point, the only question will be whether people want to exchange their Bitcoin for Euros at all or stick with the new gold money.

The scarcity is accompanied by the *platform effect*: The more participants there are in a network, the more valuable it becomes - just think of the Internet giants Amazon, Google and Facebook. Started as small projects, they grew bigger and bigger until they finally became the giants they are today.

Increasing acceptance will also spur all these effects. One is welcome to let one's gaze wander to other international countries here. The Central American country El Salvador, for example, started to top up its state reserves with Bitcoin in the summer of 2021. It is only probable that other countries will also realize that they have to look for alternatives in the financial system. The run on the last remaining Bitcoins will probably not be long in coming.

And there is still room for improvement, also with regard to the Bitcoin's value storage function. Currently, Bitcoin already has 10 percent of the market capitalization of gold. If people gradually realize that Bitcoin is the better gold, a shift in assets is will not be unlikely here.

There's no denying it: The world and the digital economy need digital money and digital gold. And one that is independent of states and cannot be used as a political weapon like the U.S. dollar. A gold money standard that is decentralized and gives people back a piece of their independence: Bitcoin.

So now the million dollar question: how will the prices of Bitcoin and Ether develop? Before we get started, a quick note: I base my predictions, in addition to the economic facts listed above, on the stock-to-flow model first applied to Bitcoin by Bitcoiner PlanB. It describes the scarcity of a good and calculates the price based on this scarcity. This model has already been able to forecast the price well in the past. Given the moment, there is nothing to say that it won't be the same in the future.

In the short-term development, I consider a Bitcoin price between 60. and 80,000 Euros likely for 2021. Compared to September 2021, that would correspond to a price increase of 50 to 100 percent. The Ether price, in turn, should move between 5,000 and 7,000 Euros at the end of 2021.

In the medium term, i.e. by the next halving, I trust the Bitcoin price to increase to between 120,000 and 150,000 Euros, and I see the Ether price between 10,000 and 12,000 Euros.

But these are forecasts - of course you can't rely on them one hundred percent, even I haven't found the crystal ball yet. Because: "Nothing is more difficult than forecasts. Especially when they concern the future." - as it is so aptly said in a bon môt.

Nevertheless, according to all the factors we have learned from in this book, such price increases are not unlikely.

But even if my forecast should be too confident and the increases should turn out to be smaller, an entry with a small to medium amount would already make a lot of sense. Because more than ever, and here I will quote Victor Hugo, "Nothing is so powerful as an idea, whose time has come."

Investments – My Plan for the Future

Even though things have gone well for me in the past, as a die-hard "Bitcoiner" I will continue to stay on the ball. That's because the insights I have made in the course of researching and engaging with this book have convinced me even more to keep investing. Here I also want to tell you what my investment plan is.

Between 40 and 50 percent of my investment in Bitcoin and Ether so far is sitting on my cold wallet, not being touched. This is where I'm going to hodln. And without ifs and buts, come what may! Because I firmly believe in the superiority of blockchain technology and the benefits of distributed ledger technologies. I think that this is a revolution in money that will change the economy and society in a big way. And as both Bitcoin and Ether become more valuable, it would be crazy to touch crypto reserves.

I have the rest of my crypto holdings spread across various exchanges. Here, I try to sell some after quick highs and get back in on the following dips - a principle also known as "ride the wave" or "wave riding". With this principle, I have been able to achieve slightly better results in the past than with hodln. Whereas with pure hodln it was just under 700 percent profit, with active managing I could easily rake in over 700 percent profits. However, when I consider the time and nerves I lost in the process, it was actually more of a losing proposition.

I also started a fund at the crypto exchange Iconomi. Its name "Risk&Safety" is program: two thirds consist of Bitcoin and Ether (Safety) and one third consists of the admixture of coins from new trend areas like the DeFi sector.

And so I close this chapter and with it the book you have in your hands. I hope you can benefit from my insights and thus have to make a lot fewer mistakes than I did when I first entered the confusing crypto world. And I also hope that you can now make a good, well-considered entry into the world of cryptocurrencies.

I wish you good luck with it, your "Cryptomaxx".

Maximilian Erlmeier

Epilogue: Social Impact and Humane Market Economy

A small postscript at the end. Even if it sometimes seems so, Satoshi Nakamoto was not concerned with filthy lucre and price increases. And even if the increases in value are pleasing for investors, that is not the most important thing about Bitcoin.

More important is the impact Bitcoin can have on people. It represents a great deal of freedom and independence through the participation of all people in the economic process and the elimination of intermediaries.

All financial transactions should be peer-to-peer, that is, person-to-person. Decentralized, worldwide, without barriers and permits, on top of that a gold money anchor and a protection against inflation - that is Bitcoin. Its spread will make the financial system more democratic, and therefore more human.

> **International remittances, often made by migrant workers back home, are currently worth an estimated $50 trillion. On average, there are 7 percent costs and fees that go into the coffers of financial service providers. Bitcoin could benefit these people.**

And just like the financial system, the social market economy is in need of repair. That's why, around the same time that Satoshi Nakamoto launched the Bitcoin revolution, I myself introduced the concept of a "humane market economy" into the discussion. Since then, we have been promoting this with the Freiburger Denkfabrik e.V. We, too, are concerned with freedom, independence and improved opportunities for success and life. In the following I still print with kind permission of BTC-ECHO an article by David Scheider, which makes the point clear, why the "Humane

Martktwirtschaft" (the humane market economy) and Bitcoin fit together.

"Inflation Is an Evil" - How the Humane Market Economy and Bitcoin Go Together
By David Scheider. Published on BTC-ECHO on July 17, 2021.

Whether you think Bitcoin is good or not depends on your point of view. Especially for followers:inside of a lesser known school of thought, BTC could be an important part in the theory framework: We are talking about the human market economy.

What would it be like to live in a world built on Bitcoin? For many a follower of the Austrian school of economics, it would be the completion of an economic utopia. A liberation from what they see as the totalitarian pretensions of central banks and fiat coercion. Admittedly, this sounds extreme.

One does not have to share this attitude toward the state money structure to recognize that fiat money need not be the last word in truth. Other schools of economic thought also take their cue from the Bitcoin idea and definitely see potential for a better and fairer world in digital gold. One of these schools of thought is the human market economy. This is a tradition that builds on both the social market economy and humanism and promotes a holistic and sustainable economic model.

Proponents of this school of thought believe that the ideal of the social market economy is no longer the right compass to navigate economies through impending crises such as climate change and social inequality. An update is needed, voila: The Human Market Economy was born.

In its structure, it is probably most comparable to ordoliberalism in the tradition of the Freiburg economists around Walter Eucken. Instead of redistribution and strong state intervention, ordoliberalism calls for the greatest possible freedom for economic actors - naturally within a set of rules laid down for this purpose by the state. Only in this way can fair economic competition be created and the political freedom of citizens be guaranteed.

The Four Pillars of the Humane Market Economy

The humane market economy builds on this concept, but brings a number of additional principles into the equation alongside the politically set framework. In concrete terms, the humane market economy is based on four pillars: 1. education, 2. regulatory framework, 3. landscape of values and 4. humanism and the image of man.

The first pillar already reveals that the individual is at the center of consideration. For theoreticians of the human market economy, it is clear that education is the key to a self-determined life. The state should therefore invest less resources in social compensation and more in education. This would make self-realization and economic freedom possible for everyone.

When it comes to the regulatory framework, the humane market economy uses classic motifs of ordoliberalism according to Walter Eucken and Franz Böhm. The state enables economic competition, but also intervenes when monopolies or oligopolies form. In a humane market economy, people enjoy all the opportunities that this entails, but they must also be liable for their actions.

Unlike ordoliberalism, however, the human market economy is based on a clear ethical framework. Thus, actors do not operate in a value-free space, but are guided by ideals such as humanity, personal responsibility and solidarity. The sustainability of economic activity also plays a key role in the humane market economy. Anarcho-capitalist ideas, such as those held by many a Bitcoiner, are therefore not congruent with the ideals of the humane market economy.

The name given to this theoretical economic order is Humanism. For the Humane Market Economy, the human being is at the center of consideration - with all his complexity. The human market economy rejects homo economicus as the basic assumption of economics; at the end of the day, the question is: How can the modern industrialized economy be given a functional and humane order?

And what does this have to do with Bitcoin?

One of the spokesmen for the humane market economy is Maximilian Erlmeier, who is an entrepreneur in the brewing industry - and quite successful. For him, it is clear that the social market economy has failed and that a rethink is needed.

In an interview with BTC-ECHO, Erlmeier also highlights the special importance of Bitcoin for a fair and self-determined life.

"Bitcoin is a way to create wealth for many. I believe that Bitcoin will lead to many people taking their finances into their own hands in the future," Maximilian Erlmeier told BTC-ECHO.

No real freedom without Bitcoin

The freedom aspect in particular weighs heavily for Erlmeier. Especially in the aspect of financial inclusion, the importance of a decentralized money becomes clear. After all, who gets a bank account and who doesn't is decided by privately driven actors such as banks. But how is the maxim of the social market economy, "prosperity for all," to be possible if there is not even rudimentary access to the financial system? This is where Bitcoin can help, Erleimer said:

"Nowadays, many areas of life are out of people's hands. You're dependent on getting a bank account or a loan." Maximilian Erlmeier in conversation with BTC-ECHO.

But inflation is also a thorn in the side of the theorists of a humane market economy. How is self-determination to be possible if people cannot even determine what they use every day, namely their money? Attentive readers of this publication should already have noticed that Bitcoiners are no friends of demonetization. Neither is Erlmeier.

"Inflation is an evil that has always existed and will always exist." Even thousands of years ago, it was common practice to successively reduce the gold content of coins, Erlmeier says.

"This just shows that the one who has the monopoly over money creation is committing dirty tricks with this privilege and expropriating savers," he says. This observation could not be more timely: just recently, the ECB raised its inflation target from "close to but below 2 percent" to two percent.

Acknowledgements

A book doesn't come out of nowhere. There are many influences that contribute to the letters finding their way onto paper.

Reading good reference books, discussions and newsletters gave me the background knowledge to start writing. Attending seminars, professional conferences and conventions, have also helped me a lot, as well as my experiences from 45 years of professional life. Both as an employee of large corporations and as a boss of medium-sized companies and as a consultant, I was able to gather important experience that has found its way into this book in one form or another.

But what contributes most to the creation of a book are people. That is why I would like to express my heartfelt thanks to the following people and organizations:

The online magazine BTC-ECHO with its editor-in-chief Sven Wagenknecht, as well as David Scheider, whose article on the "Human Market Economy" is part of this book.

Special thanks go to the physicist and risk manager Dr. Laurids Schimka. He told me about Bitcoin, introduced me to the subject, coached me, and provided me with advice and support. Thanks to him I am a Bitcoiner today!

A big thank you also goes to my daughter Miriam, who helped me with ideas, advice and hints during the creation of these pages.

And most of all, of course, to Phillip Horch, freelance writer and connoisseur of the crypto scene. He put most of my ideas and rough drafts into shape, added more chapters, and significantly shaped the book through discussions, suggestions, and editorial work. Thank you!

Last but not least: Maurice Batras, who designed the cover and the graphics.

Disclaimer

This book has been researched and written with the utmost care - nevertheless, no guarantee can be made as to the accuracy and completeness of the information presented. In addition, the statements dealing with possible investments are in no way recommendations for action, these pages do not constitute investment advice. They are not invitations to purchase or sell specific digital currencies in the sense of investment advice or brokerage. The author is not liable for any financial losses that may occur. Without being obliged to do so, I point out that any investment in digital assets is speculative and thus both opportunities but also risks of loss up to total loss of the invested capital can arise.

Bitcoin: A Peer-to-Peer Electronic Cash System

Satoshi Nakamoto

satoshin@gmx.com

www.bitcoin.org

Abstract. A purely peer-to-peer version of electronic cash would allow online payments to be sent directly from one party to another without going through a financial institution. Digital signatures provide part of the solution, but the main benefits are lost if a trusted third party is still required to prevent double-spending.

We propose a solution to the double-spending problem using a peer-to-peer network.

The network timestamps transactions by hashing them into an ongoing chain of hash-based proof-of-work, forming a record that cannot be changed without redoing the proof-of-work. The longest chain not only serves as proof of the sequence of events witnessed, but proof that it came from the largest pool of CPU power. As long as a majority of CPU power is controlled by nodes that are not cooperating to attack the network, they'll generate the longest chain and outpace attackers. The network itself requires minimal structure. Messages are broadcast on a best effort basis, and nodes can leave and rejoin the network at will, accepting the longest proof-of-work chain as proof of what happened while they were gone.

1. Introduction

Commerce on the Internet has come to rely almost exclusively on financial institutions serving as trusted third parties to process electronic payments. While the system works well enough for most transactions, it still suffers from the inherent weaknesses of the trust based model.

Completely non-reversible transactions are not really possible, since financial institutions cannot avoid mediating disputes. The cost of mediation increases transaction costs, limiting the minimum practical transaction size and cutting off the possibility for small casual transactions, and there is a broader cost in the loss of ability to make non-reversible payments for non-reversible services. With the possibility of reversal, the need for trust spreads. Merchants must be wary of their customers, hassling them for more information than they would otherwise need.

A certain percentage of fraud is accepted as unavoidable. These costs and payment uncertainties can be avoided in person by using physical currency, but no mechanism exists to make payments over a communications channel without a trusted party.

What is needed is an electronic payment system based on cryptographic proof instead of trust, allowing any two willing parties to transact directly with each other without the need for a trusted third party. Transactions that are computationally impractical to reverse would protect sellers from fraud, and routine escrow mechanisms could easily be implemented to protect buyers. In this paper, we propose a solution to the double-spending problem using a peer-to-peer distributed timestamp server to generate computational proof of the chronological order of transactions. The system is secure as long as honest nodes collectively control more CPU power than any cooperating group of attacker nodes.

2. Transactions

We define an electronic coin as a chain of digital signatures. Each owner transfers the coin to the next by digitally signing a hash of the previous transaction and the public key of the next owner and adding these to the end of the coin. A payee can verify the signatures to verify the chain of ownership.

The problem of course is the payee can't verify that one of the owners did not double-spend the coin. A common solution is to introduce a trusted central authority, or mint, that checks every transaction for double spending. After each transaction, the coin must be returned to the mint to issue a new coin, and only coins issued directly from the mint arge trusted not to be double-spent.

The problem with this solution is that the fate of the entire money system depends on the company running the mint, with every transaction having to go through them, just like a bank.

We need a way for the payee to know that the previous owners did not sign any earlier transactions. For our purposes, the earliest transaction is the one that counts, so we don't care about later attempts to double-spend. The only way to confirm the absence of a transaction is to be aware of all transactions. In the mint based model, the mint was aware of all transactions and decided which arrived first. To accomplish this without a trusted party, transactions must be

publicly announced, and we need a system for participants to agree on a single history of the order in which they were received. The payee needs proof that at the time of each transaction, the majority of nodes agreed it was the first received.

3. Timestamp Server

The solution we propose begins with a timestamp server. A timestamp server works by taking a hash of a block of items to be timestamped and widely publishing the hash, such as in a newspaper or Usenet post [2-5]. The timestamp proves that the data must have existed at the time, obviously, in order to get into the hash. Each timestamp includes the previous timestamp in its hash, forming a chain, with each additional timestamp reinforcing the ones before it.

4. Proof-of-Work

To implement a distributed timestamp server on a peer-to-peer basis, we will need to use a proof-of-work system similar to Adam Back's Hashcash [6], rather than newspaper or Usenet posts.

The proof-of-work involves scanning for a value that when hashed, such as with SHA-256, the hash begins with a number of zero bits. The average work required is exponential in the number of zero bits required and can be verified by executing a single hash.

For our timestamp network, we implement the proof-of-work by incrementing a nonce in the block until a value is found that gives the block's hash the required zero bits. Once the CPU effort has been expended to make it satisfy the proof-of-work, the block cannot be changed without redoing the work. As later blocks are chained after it, the work to change the block would include redoing all the blocks after it.

The proof-of-work also solves the problem of determining representation in majority decision making. If the majority were based on one-IP-address-one-vote, it could be subverted by anyone able to allocate many IPs. Proof-of-work is essentially one-CPU-one-vote. The majority decision is represented by the longest chain, which has the greatest proof-of-work effort invested in it. If a majority of CPU power is controlled by honest nodes, the honest chain will grow the fastest and outpace any competing chains. To modify a past block, an attacker would have to redo the proof-of-work of the block and all blocks after it and then catch up with and surpass the work of the honest nodes. We will show later that the probability of a slower attacker catching up diminishes exponentially as subsequent blocks are added.

To compensate for increasing hardware speed and varying interest in running nodes over time, the proof-of-work difficulty is determined by a moving average targeting an average number of blocks per hour. If they're generated too fast, the difficulty increases.

5. Network

The steps to run the network are as follows:

1) New transactions are broadcast to all nodes.

2) Each node collects new transactions into a block.

3) Each node works on finding a difficult proof-of-work for its block.

4) When a node finds a proof-of-work, it broadcasts the block to all nodes.

5) Nodes accept the block only if all transactions in it are valid and not already spent.

6) Nodes express their acceptance of the block by working on creating the next block in the chain, using the hash of the accepted block as the previous hash.

Nodes always consider the longest chain to be the correct one and will keep working on extending it. If two nodes broadcast different versions of the next block simultaneously, some nodes may receive one or the other first. In that case, they work on the first one they received, but save the other branch in case it becomes longer. The tie will be broken when the next proof-of-work is found and one branch becomes longer; the nodes that were working on the other branch will then switch to the longer one.

Block

Prev Hash Nonce

Tx Tx ...

Block

Prev Hash Nonce

Tx Tx ...

New transaction broadcasts do not necessarily need to reach all nodes. As long as they reach many nodes, they will get into a block before long. Block broadcasts are also tolerant of dropped messages. If a node does not receive a block, it will request it when it receives the next block and realizes it missed one.

6. Incentive

By convention, the first transaction in a block is a special transaction that starts a new coin owned by the creator of the block. This adds an incentive for nodes to support the network, and provides a way to initially distribute coins into circulation, since there is no central authority to issue them.

The steady addition of a constant of amount of new coins is analogous to gold miners expending resources to add gold to circulation. In our case, it is CPU time and electricity that is expended.

The incentive can also be funded with transaction fees. If the output value of a transaction is less than its input value, the difference is a transaction fee that is added to the incentive value of the block containing the transaction. Once a predetermined number of coins have entered circulation, the incentive can transition entirely to transaction fees and be completely inflation free.

The incentive may help encourage nodes to stay honest. If a greedy attacker is able to assemble more CPU power than all the honest nodes, he would have to choose between using it to defraud people by stealing back his payments, or using it to generate new coins. He ought to find it more profitable to play by the rules, such rules that favour him with more new coins than everyone else combined, than to undermine the system and the validity of his own wealth.

7. Reclaiming Disk Space

Once the latest transaction in a coin is buried under enough blocks, the spent transactions before it can be discarded to save disk space. To facilitate this without breaking the block's hash, transactions are hashed in a Merkle Tree [7][2][5], with only the root included in the block's hash.

Old blocks can then be compacted by stubbing off branches of the tree. The interior hashes do not need to be stored.

A block header with no transactions would be about 80 bytes. If we suppose blocks are generated every 10 minutes, 80 bytes * 6 * 24 * 365 = 4.2MB per year. With computer systems typically selling with 2GB of RAM as of 2008, and Moore's Law predicting current growth of 1.2GB per year, storage should not be a problem even if the block headers must be kept in memory.

BlockBlock Block Header (Block Hash)

Prev Hash Nonce

Hash01

Hash0 Hash1 Hash2Hash3

Hash23

Root Hash

Hash01

Hash2

Tx3

Hash23

Block Header (Block Hash)

Root Hash

Transactions Hashed in a Merkle Tree After Pruning Tx0-2 from the Block

Prev Hash Nonce

Hash3

Tx0 Tx1 Tx2Tx3

8. Simplified Payment Verification

It is possible to verify payments without running a full network node. A user only needs to keep a copy of the block headers of the longest proof-of-work chain, which he can get by querying network nodes until he's convinced he has the longest chain, and obtain the Merkle branch linking the transaction to the block it's timestamped in. He can't check the transaction for himself, but by linking it to a place in the chain, he can see that a network node has accepted it, and blocks added after it further confirm the network has accepted it.

As such, the verification is reliable as long as honest nodes control the network, but is more vulnerable if the network is overpowered by an attacker. While network nodes can verify transactions for themselves, the simplified method can be fooled by an attacker's fabricated transactions for as long as the attacker can continue to overpower the network. One strategy to protect against this would be to accept alerts from network nodes when they detect an invalid block, prompting the user's software to download the full block and alerted transactions to confirm the inconsistency. Businesses that receive frequent payments will probably still want to run their own nodes for more independent security and quicker verification.

9. Combining and Splitting Value

Although it would be possible to handle coins individually, it would be unwieldy to make a separate transaction for every cent in a transfer. To allow value to be split and combined, transactions contain multiple inputs and outputs. Normally there will be either a single input from a larger previous transaction or multiple inputs combining smaller amounts, and at most two outputs: one for the payment, and one returning the change, if any, back to the sender.

It should be noted that fan-out, where a transaction depends on several transactions, and those transactions depend on many more, is not a problem here. There is never the need to extract a complete standalone copy of a transaction's history.

Transaction

In

...

In Out

...

Hash01

Hash2Hash3

Hash23

Block Header

Merkle Root

Prev Hash Nonce

Block Header

Merkle Root

Prev Hash Nonce

Block Header

Merkle Root

Prev Hash Nonce

Merkle Branch for Tx3

Tx3

10. Privacy

The traditional banking model achieves a level of privacy by limiting access to information to the parties involved and the trusted third party. The necessity to announce all transactions publicly precludes this method, but privacy can still be maintained by breaking the flow of information in another place: by keeping public keys anonymous. The public can see that someone is sending an amount to someone else, but without information linking the transaction to anyone. This is similar to the level of information released by stock exchanges, where the time and size of individual trades, the "tape", is made public, but without telling who the parties were.

As an additional firewall, a new key pair should be used for each transaction to keep them from being linked to a common owner. Some linking is still unavoidable with multi-input transactions, which necessarily reveal that their inputs were owned by the same owner. The risk is that if the owner of a key is revealed, linking could reveal other transactions that belonged to the same owner.

11. Calculations

We consider the scenario of an attacker trying to generate an alternate chain faster than the honest chain. Even if this is accomplished, it does not throw the system open to arbitrary changes, such as creating value out of thin air or taking money that never belonged to the attacker. Nodes are not going to accept an invalid transaction as payment, and honest nodes will never accept a block containing them. An attacker can only try to change one of his own transactions to take back money he recently spent.

The race between the honest chain and an attacker chain can be characterized as a Binomial Random Walk. The success event is the honest chain being extended by one block, increasing its lead by +1, and the failure event is the attacker's chain being extended by one block, reducing the

gap by -1.

The probability of an attacker catching up from a given deficit is analogous to a Gambler's Ruin problem. Suppose a gambler with unlimited credit starts at a deficit and plays potentially an infinite number of trials to try to reach breakeven. We can calculate the probability he ever

reaches breakeven, or that an attacker ever catches up with the honest chain, as follows [8]:

p = probability an honest node finds the next block

q = probability the attacker finds the next block

qz = probability the attacker will ever catch up from z blocks behind

$q_z = \{1$ if $p \le q$

$\Box q/p\Box z$ if $p\Box q\}$

6

Identities Transactions Trusted

Third Party Counterparty Public

Identities Transactions Public

New Privacy Model

Traditional Privacy Model

Given our assumption that $p > q$, the probability drops exponentially as the number of blocks the attacker has to catch up with increases. With the odds against him, if he doesn't make a lucky lunge forward early on, his chances become vanishingly small as he falls further behind.

We now consider how long the recipient of a new transaction needs to wait before being sufficiently certain the sender can't change the transaction. We assume the sender is an attacker who wants to make the recipient believe he paid him for a while, then switch it to pay back to himself after some time has passed. The receiver will be alerted when that happens, but the sender hopes it will be too late.

The receiver generates a new key pair and gives the public key to the sender shortly before signing. This prevents the sender from preparing a chain of blocks ahead of time by working on it continuously until he is lucky enough to get far enough ahead, then executing the transaction at that moment. Once the transaction is sent, the dishonest sender starts working in secret on a parallel chain containing an alternate version of his transaction.

The recipient waits until the transaction has been added to a block and z blocks have been linked after it. He doesn't know the exact amount of progress the attacker has made, but assuming the honest blocks took the average expected time per block, the attacker's potential progress will be a Poisson distribution with expected value:

$$\lambda = z \frac{q}{p}$$

To get the probability the attacker could still catch up now, we multiply the Poisson density for each amount of progress he could have made by the probability he could catch up from that point:

$$\sum k = 0$$

$$\infty \square k \ e - \square$$

$$k ! \cdot \{ \square q / p \square \square z - k \square \ if \ k \leq z$$

1 if k $\square$ z}Rearranging to avoid summing the infinite tail of the distribution…

$$1 - \sum k = 0$$

$$z \square k \ e - \square$$

$$k! \square 1 - \square q / p \square \square z - k \square \square \ .$$

Converting to C code...

```c
#include <math.h>

double AttackerSuccessProbability(double q, int z)

{

double p = 1.0 - q;

double lambda = z * (q / p);

double sum = 1.0;

int i, k;

for (k = 0; k <= z; k++)

{

double poisson = exp(-lambda);
```

```
for (i = 1; i <= k; i++)

poisson *= lambda / i;

sum -= poisson * (1 - pow(q / p, z - k));

}

return sum;

}
```

7

Running some results, we can see the probability drop off exponentially with z.

© 2021, Maximilian Erlmeier
Herstellung und Verlag: BoD – Books
on Demand, Norderstedt
ISBN: 9783755736233

Sources

Andreas Antonopoulos: Mastering Ethereum: Building Smart Contracts and DApps, Online-Publikation, 2018.

BTC-ECHO: www.btc-echo.de; www.btc-academy.de

Cambridge Bitcoin Energy Consumption Index: https://cbeci.org/index

Fabian Schär und Aleksander Berentsen: Bitcoin, Blockchain und Kryptoassets: Eine umfassende Einführung. Universität Basel, Basel, 2017.

René Sedillot: Muscheln, Münzen und Papier. Die Geschichte des Geldes. Frankfurt/New York, 1992, ISBN 3-593-34707-5.

Worldbank: www.wordbank.org